F.A. MANN

A MEMOIR

F.A. Mann

A Memoir

Geoffrey Lewis

*for Xandra
with love from
Geoffrey*

·HART·
PUBLISHING

OXFORD AND PORTLAND, OREGON
2013

Published in the United Kingdom by Hart Publishing Ltd
16C Worcester Place, Oxford, OX1 2JW
Telephone: +44 (0)1865 517530
Fax: +44 (0)1865 510710
E-mail: mail@hartpub.co.uk
Website: http://www.hartpub.co.uk

Published in North America (US and Canada) by
Hart Publishing
c/o International Specialized Book Services
920 NE 58th Avenue, Suite 300
Portland, OR 97213-3786
USA
Tel: +1 503 287 3093 or toll-free: (1) 800 944 6190
Fax: +1 503 280 8832
E-mail: orders@isbs.com
Website: http://www.isbs.com

© Geoffrey M Lewis 2013

British Library Cataloguing in Publication Data
Data Available

ISBN: 978-184946-563-2

Typeset by Criteria International
Printed and bound in Great Britain by
TJ International Ltd, Padstow, Cornwall

Preface

Francis Mann came from Germany and became one of the most distinguished practitioners and writers in English law of his generation, and an international lawyer of world-wide reputation. He combined a flourishing practice with a prodigious output of teaching and writing. That is to say he was a jurist, which is rare in the legal profession in England. It is rarer still to find one who had had a legal training in Germany as well as a life in the law in England. Francis' knowledge of both the English and continental legal systems enriched all his work.

When in 1958 he joined the partnership of Herbert Smith & Co., of which I was then a junior member, I realised little of all this and did not have more than an inkling of how fortunate we all were going to be. Within days of his arrival I was plunged into a heavy case that he was conducting, with the trial only weeks away. One of the senior silks he had briefed for the trial told me that I was in for an exciting time. No prediction could have been more to the point. After more than thirty years of working closely with him, during which time he became my mentor and friend as well as my partner, my abiding impression is that he carried the life force within him every day until his death in 1991. What is the news? he would demand almost daily. If you had none you would feel that somehow you were failing. But if you had a new case, he would transform it. You had only to sketch the outline facts for him to seize on its essential features and imbue it with energy and infectious excitement.

This short book is not a study of his contribution to, and influence upon English legal thinking and practice. That has been admirably done by Lawrence Collins who, as a jurist too, is Francis Mann's heir. I gratefully acknowledge my debt to his writings. This memoir is a personal recollection of a remarkable man and lawyer. There are however parts of his life that I did not or could not know: his early life in Germany until it was destroyed by Hitler, his first difficult years in London and his crucial visit to Berlin in 1946. For these I have been able to draw on a variety of sources: his own writings and his letters to his wife, Lore, and the memories of their three children, David, Jessica and Nicola, and of his many friends and colleagues in England and Germany. To all those who have helped me I am more than grateful. I could not have written this book without them. I am also indebted to Claudia von der Brüggen for her generously-given help with the German aspects of Francis Mann's life and with some translations from the German. I am grateful to Anne Kriken Mann, David Mann's widow, for permission to quote from Francis' own writings and letters. Finally I thank Richard Hart for his support and confidence in bringing the book to the public.

Towards the end of his life Francis Mann revealed
that he had been inspired by a passage in a letter from
Turgenev to Tolstoy which he had come across when he
was a boy. It had, he said, pursued him and served as a
leitmotiv all his life.

Humanität ist kein leeres Wort. Lasst Euch nichts weismachen
von den Maulaufreissern dieser trübseligen Epoche, von den
Amokläufern, den Veitstänzern und heulenden Derwischen
irgendwelcher Bekenntnisse. Wahr sein, einfach sein,
milden Herzens sein, heiter und gelassen bleiben in Leiden
und Gefahr, das Leben lieben und den Tod nicht fürchen,
dem Geist dienen und an Geister nicht glauben, – es ist doch
nichts besseres gelehrt worden, seitdem die Erde sich dreht.

Humanity is not an empty word. Do not be fooled by big
talkers of this sad period, by those who run amok, St Vitus
dancers and howling dervishes. Be honest, be simple, be
serene and calm when in pain or danger, love life and do
not fear death, serve the spirit and do not believe in ghosts.
Nothing better has been taught since the earth began to turn.

Francis Mann
as a boy

Francis as a young man

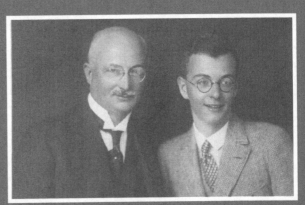

Francis Mann
with his
father and
grandfather

Francis Mann with his father

Lore and
Francis

Lore and
Francis

Lore and Francis

Francis Mann with the Belgian team during the hearings in the Barcelona Traction Case, 1969.
First row: from left, Maître Marcel Grégoire, Professor Michel Virally, Elihu Lauterpacht QC (later Professor Sir Elihu Lauterpacht QC.) Francis Mann.
Second row: Professor Michel Waelbroeck, John Kirkpatrick (later Professor John Kirkpatrick), Lawrence Collins (later Lord Collins of Mapesbury).

Francis Mann

Contents

I

Frankenthal

Frankenthal: a small town in the Palatinate region a few miles north of Mannheim, lying at a little distance from the west bank of the Rhine astride the road going south from Worms to Speyer. Further west the country rolls a little and the slopes are covered by neatly trained vines producing the excellent Pfalz wines. To the south the great conurbation of Mannheim and Ludwigshafen; to the east the river flows up through the industrial heartland to the sea. The town itself has a lifeless air. Its streets exhale the monotony of a provincial German town. Its name suggests that it had once been part of France. For this west bank has been fought over again and again by French and German.

In the corner of one of the quiet streets is a large house without attractive features. Westliche Ringstrasse 19. Here, in the early years of the twentieth century, Richard Mann lived and practised law from a modest office down the street. Although the town was small there was good enough reason for him to choose it. Its importance might have declined under competition from the cities and the vast sprawling chemical factories nearby, but it remained an important legal centre. It was home to the District Court of one of the richest regions of South Germany. It was also the headquarters of the family banking firm whose fortunes had been founded on the local wine trade.

Photographs of Richard Mann show a heavy face with something unyielding about the eyes. That was certainly true of the rock-like ethic by which he lived – professional and personal. There was not much laughter about him. His wife Ida suffered a breakdown when their only child was very young and spent the rest of her life, some 25 years, in an institution. According to the custom of the day, the subject was not talked about. Her elder sister Laura was then *Fraulein* teaching German at Hamilton House, a school in Tunbridge Wells. Richard asked her to return to Germany to keep house for him and help him bring up the small boy. The *Hamiltonian* for Easter Term 1911 said in its valedictory note that she was "obliged to go home, as her only sister was very delicate and longed for her society and care." She answered the call at once without demur, and stayed with Richard until he died in Oxford in 1953.

Both Richard and Ida were from Jewish families who had long been living in the country on either side of the Rhine. His forbears are recorded as having lived in the Palatinate district since at latest the second half of the eighteenth century; and the family banking house of Mann and Loeb had been first entered in the commercial register in Frankenthal in 1863, established by Richard's grandfather and his cousin. Richard had a promising academic career and read law at several German universities, qualifying finally at Munich high in the list of successful candidates. At school he formed a lifelong friendship with Karl Helfferich who became a well-known economist and was nominated for the Presidency of the Reichsbank, although not appointed. Helfferich's special subject was money and he wrote a celebrated treatise which was cited as a source in each successive edition of Francis Mann's own "Legal Aspect of Money".

Ida's maiden name was Oppenheim and her family can be traced back in a book on the history of the Jewish community in Bonn as far as the end of the seventeenth century. Both Ida's parents died while she was in her teens and she and her sister were brought up by their mother's brother, Franz Cohen, until they went to a finishing school in Bonn. Cohen was a remarkable man whom Francis Mann remembered. His abiding interest was the music of Mozart, and he was one of the founders, perhaps the moving spirit of the Mozarteum in Salzburg.

Richard Mann was studying law at Bonn when he met Ida. As their son wrote in an unpublished memoir, Richard fell violently in love with her. "She must have been very beautiful and attractive. This made him wish to marry her at the earliest possible moment. But he could not expect to establish a practice with the speed he needed to found a family at any place other than his home town and so in 1898 or so he opened his office at Frankenthal." They married in 1900 in Cologne and had one child born on 11th August 1907.

These two families that were joined in marriage were settled and established. As Jews they were emancipated, for Germany in the first years of the twentieth century was the European country where Jews could feel most at home. It was a golden period of imagination and achievement in the arts. Society respected the intellect. Everywhere Jews played a prominent part. There were, as always, instances of discrimination but Mann himself remembered no single unpleasant incident in his early life directed against him. Families of assimilated Jews like Richard and Ida did not parade their Jewishness and were often non-observant. Many of them fought for Germany in the first war. Richard believed in the rightness of his country's cause and joined up at the end of the war. Little in that time hinted at what was to come.

The child who was born to Richard and Ida was Friedrich August Alexander Mann, an only child known always as Fritz. An aunt, Laura, stood in for the absent mother. The boy learned to pursue the interior life of the only child. His best friend was an imaginary character called Fleming, with whom he could indulge his dreams. Laura was a good and motherly woman with a warm personality who devoted herself for the rest of her life to making a home for her brother-in-law and bringing up his child. There was also a housekeeper and nanny, Lydia, who was not Jewish. Mann looked her up after the war, nearly forty years later, and found that she had not changed.

Richard Mann was a man of this world. His influence, a very potent one, was to bring on in his son the early maturity which anyway is the tendency of an only child. He was not an easy man: moody and often depressed, he could make unreasonable demands or descend into sarcasm. These foibles were very fairly accounted for by the son as the by-products of a hard life that had been dogged by misfortune. But Richard was also a man of culture who kept up the interests which his classical education had implanted. He knew by heart much of Goethe and Schiller, and travelled to Berlin and other cities for concerts and plays. He had the intelligent lawyer's interest in politics and the usual horror of getting himself involved in it.

Francis Mann admired his father unqualifiedly. But what surprised him at an early age was his complete lack of ambition. Here was a cultured man of outstanding intelligence, with great qualities as a lawyer, but who never sought a larger or more prominent field for himself than the narrow confines of Frankenthal. The affection that the boy had for his father was tinged with respect, or to use his own rather chilling word – awe. "I owe him more than I can realise", he wrote later. "I owe him the standards which have decisively influenced my own life and my attitude towards people and things. I owe him the unbending professional integrity which frequently quite unconsciously and incidentally he taught and impressed on me." Words to be weighed. In that lonely and austere childhood there would have been the terror of what had happened to the mother who had been taken away from him without warning and before the age of understanding. Yet the boy apparently imbibed his father's demanding lessons that would give him the resource to weather the disappointment and disaster that lay ahead.

From an early age he used to call for his father at the end of the working day and they would take a walk together. Richard talked about the law and its practice. The boy soon knew that he wanted to become a lawyer. Everything he learned encouraged him and later on he spent time in his father's office. Working with his father and talking to him constantly taught him not only about law but also etiquette: what was done and not done and the nature of professional integrity. He considered that nothing that he learned at university was as useful, and he could never understand the English habit of insulating children from their father's office work. If a man loved his work it should be natural for him to want to show it to his children. He also learned something else from his father that could not be had from text books – forensic tactics. When he became an English solicitor his reputation in litigation depended a good deal on his mastery of court procedure and the often decisive advantage which can be seized during the preliminary skirmishes before the set piece of the trial.

At the weekends father and son went for longer walks in the wine country. Wine was important. Richard had a reputation for his knowledge of the legal aspects of wine production. Every meal at home was accompanied by wine, and the wine cellar was carefully stocked and added to after much deliberation each autumn.

The young Fritz met well known lawyers who were involved in his father's cases and absorbed their talk and their style. His father's style, above all, was the influence that lasted for the rest of his life. The little things were the most important because they were done as a matter of course, like conditioned reflexes. Mann remembered an instance. A client was accused of perjury in a case that Richard was handling. He told his son that he had done his best to stop it because a lawyer should always prevent a witness from perjuring himself if he could. Francis Mann never accepted that the lawyer's role was passive.

The young Fritz went to local day schools in Frankenthal and Ludwigshafen. He remembered the teaching as excellent and of a liberal tenor. Much of what he learned, the Latin and French especially, remained with him for the rest of his life. The pupils were worked hard and he was always at or near the top of his form: to work at anything less than full throttle would not have occurred to him. He learned the piano seriously and read voraciously, particularly the great novelists, German, English, Russian and French. His father took him occasionally to the theatre or to concerts. When he looked back to these days he did not know how it had been possible to fit everything in, but he marvelled at the fullness of the life he had been taught to lead.

He took his final examination in 1926. He was therefore living at home during the early years of the Weimar Republic. From 1919 when he was twelve the

Palatinate was occupied under the terms of the Treaty of Versailles. First Americans and then French were billeted in the maisonette in the corner house. "For years," Mann recalled, "we had M. le Comte Gary de la Garenne. He was a French royalist who served in the Republican Army, but refused to become an officer. My principal memory of him is the daily visit which during a period of many years he paid punctually at 6 p.m. to my aunt. He had himself announced, entered the room, bowed deeply and with an unforgettable movement of his arms used the standard formula: ' *Je vous presente mes compliments, Madame.*' He made polite conversation for a few minutes and retired."

Mann was 16 in 1923 when the fevered life of the Weimar Republic reached its crisis. The allies turned down the German government's request for a delay of two years on reparation payments, the crippling obligations that the victors had imposed on Germany after the war. These fell into default. The French marched into the Ruhr to enforce the payments. In January the German government declared a policy of passive resistance against the occupation of the Ruhr. In Bavaria particularly, but elsewhere in Germany as well, lawlessness gained the upper hand. In Munich Hitler made a bungled attempt to seize power. Ludendorff, one of the heroes of the war, was implicated but acquitted. The streets and beer cellars of the city were filled with armed and steel-helmeted bands of thugs. It was a glimpse of things to come. Then the German inflation that had been rising ominously ran out of control.

It was a year before the economy was again brought to order. During that year the country was in chaos. Hunger and ruin visited the poor and the middle classes. The President of the Department of Health, speaking in the

Reichstag in February 1923, gave a harrowing picture of increasing malnutrition, disease and death in the towns. Food was not available because farmers were unwilling to turn their produce into the unpredictable money. Prices rose between morning and afternoon. A barter trade developed and Richard Mann was often paid in wine or vegetables. He came home one day and announced triumphantly that he had earned a single American dollar – which was by then valued in billions of marks. The crisis passed. The currency was stabilised by the introduction of the *Rentenmark* and the reparation question was rationalised by the Dawes Plan in 1924. The plan provided for the phased payment of reparations, starting at a low level and linked to foreign loans to Germany. It seemed as if sense would prevail, until all progress was blown away by the world economic crisis of 1929.

The events of 1923 marked themselves permanently on the mind of the young Mann, particularly the consequences of runaway inflation that had destroyed a large segment of the lower and middle classes and had corrupted civilised values everywhere. He never forgot the inflation and referred to it often in later life. He had seen at first hand that morality was the first casualty of a crumbling currency. He may well have been influenced by the views of his father's friend Karl Helfferich who was one of the authors of the *Rentenmark* and had consistently argued that the value of money must be based on something more substantial than the volume of paper in circulation. In any case, Mann had seen that the simple expedient of printing more bank notes could eventually destroy a society.

II

Berlin

At Eastertime in 1926 Mann left Frankenthal for good. His father had decided that he should continue his education, as he had himself and as was the fashion in Germany, by attending several universities consecutively. He was to start by taking a term at Geneva so that he could master written and spoken French. Richard did not know that Geneva was then the most fashionable gathering point for students, at least for young Germans reading law. But he would have approved, because by spending a term there his son met and befriended many who were later to be successful and influential in the profession. A few were to become colleagues for life, but most of the friendships were lost in the Nazi years.

Mann lodged with the widow of a professor of law in the old part of the town. Two or three other students were there as well, and they conversed in French with the old lady. She was a refined, highly educated person and she insisted with the utmost rigour on *le bel usage*. It was all highly convivial and Mann considered that it was not merely the best, but the only way to learn a language properly.

It was a happy time for him. Geneva was then a charming town and the students came from all over Europe. They bicycled everywhere, swam in the lake and made trips to the mountains. They learned no law. That hardly mattered, for they made friends and learned much else, including the pleasure of talking endlessly in pavement cafes about the questions of the day. The sky was cloudless in that Swiss spring. When term ended Mann travelled through central France. He saw the chateaux of the Loire dreaming in the sunshine and stayed for a couple of months near Blois perfecting his French conversation and studying French literature, finally meeting some of his Geneva friends again for three weeks in Paris. The following summer he visited England and stayed in Oxfordshire for three months, again learning the language and conventions of another country. Was this not the best – and most pleasurable – way of preparing himself for an unknown future?

Life became altogether more serious after the Arcadian spring and summer of 1926. He spent a term in Berlin and then moved to Munich, returning to Berlin in the summer of 1928 where he stayed until he left Germany for good in 1933. He was struck by the contrast in quality between the universities of Munich and Berlin. Munich was provincial. Although some of the teaching was good, the students were too easily distracted (there was much to distract them in the Munich of the late twenties) and consequently under-achieved. The professors turned a blind eye.

It was apparent early on that, whatever he undertook, Mann would never settle for second best. Music was an instance. All his life he loved music and was a discriminating listener. It moved him as perhaps nothing else, not even a human friendship, and released emotions which he found difficult to express. While he was at school he had learned the piano with the application which was invariable for him. Then one evening while he was in Munich he heard Karl Friedberg, one of the leading pianists of the day. A great player can make a young aspirant despair. As he walked home after the concert, Mann decided, "I could never reach a standard of playing comparable to his, that it was impossible to do more than one thing perfectly (I had read something by Goethe to that effect) and that, therefore, the only sensible thing was to concentrate on law and to stop playing the piano in my inferior way. I have regretted it ever since.

Berlin was infinitely more to his taste than Munich. It was a capital city and not only in the political sense. In music, theatre, and the graphic arts creative exuberance was in the air. Some have called it a Periclean Age, but in truth the Weimar years were a brilliant sunset. There was a premonition of disaster from the beginning. As early as January 1920, Count Harry Kessler[1] noted in his diary on the day that the Treaty of Versailles was ratified in Paris that, although the war was officially over, "a terrible era begins for Europe, like the gathering of clouds before a storm, and it will end in an explosion probably still more terrible than that of the World War."

Mann lived in Berlin at a crucial point in European history. It would be decided here whether the world could remain at peace. If not, an entire civilisation would be destroyed and could never be recreated. By the time the twenties were closing the atmosphere had become febrile. The images left from those years convey this powerfully: the novels of Christopher Isherwood, the

---

[1] Count Harry Kessler: born 1868, the son of a banker ennobled by Kaiser Wilhelm I; founded the Cranach Press to publish fine editions of literary masterpieces; served in the First War and on diplomatic missions afterwards; exiled himself to Paris when Hitler came to power; died 1937. Kessler was a republican of leftward inclination who despised Nazism. He knew everyone in the worlds of art and public affairs and his diaries give a vivid picture of the doomed brilliance of the Weimar years in Germany.

art of George Grosz and the writings of Bertold Brecht. A city of grotesques with an appetite for perversion. But thinking about it much later from the perspective of fifty years, Mann considered that Isherwood's picture was partial and distorted. In his own memory, "it was a centre of research, art and academic and cultural activity such as the world has rarely seen", and he recalled that as students they participated in it to the full. At the theatre, where there seemed to be a new play every week for the comment of the great critic Alfred Kerr, the legendary Max Reinhardt was the dominant figure. Music was, he recalled, of an incomparable variety and richness. He heard orchestras under Furtwängler, Walter, Klemperer and Kleiber, and he began to be familiar with the chamber music of the Viennese classical repertory which was to become his first love. One of Mann's obituarists, Lord Hoffmann, had invited him shortly before his death to a performance of Berg's *Wozzeck*, and introduced him to the conductor, Mark Elder. Elder asked him whether he had ever seen the opera before. Yes, he replied mildly, I went to the first performance in Berlin in 1925.

He also began to interest himself in painting. The interest was fostered by the family's friendship with Justin Thannhauser, the well-known dealer and collector, from whom Richard Mann bought some Vlamincks and an Utrillo. His son always admired and loved them.

The law faculty of the Humboldt University of Berlin stood head and shoulders above any other in Germany. The tradition of Savigny, who had been the first holder of the chair in Roman law in 1810, lived on, with its tenet that the practice and theory of jurisprudence cannot be divorced without injury to both. Here Mann found the spirit of free enquiry and rigorous research which became his meat and drink. Above all he admired the "style" –

the same quality which he had found in his father, and the same quality that all his friends and colleagues were later to recognise as his own hallmark. Looking back to his time in Berlin, Mann singled out Martin Wolff as the greatest teacher he had ever known. First appointed to the Berlin law faculty in 1903 at the age of 31, he was venerated by the time Mann was taught by him, a frail hunch-backed figure whose features, Mann recalled, glowed with extraordinary intellectual force. Wolff lectured to halls crammed with students squatting on the floor or perched on window sills, listening as if under a spell. Mann recalled how Wolff gained his students' devotion:

> For a lifetime I have asked myself: how did he do it? I can say, negatively, not by jokes, not by cheap witticisms or asides, not by histrionics, not by false pathos, not by shouting or even by raising his voice. He did it by the authority and at the same time the simplicity of his personality, by the devotion to his educational task, by the obvious genuineness of his wish not to hear himself speak, but to force the students to follow his line of thought.

Wolff had written on the subject of money as long before as 1917. In the obituary notice that Mann wrote after Wolff's death in England in 1953, published in the *Journal du Droit International*, he referred to the article, describing it as "a contribution of fundamental and universal importance to the legal theory of money in general."[2] Naturally Mann drew on his master's work in his own book on Money. Wolff came to England as a refugee in 1938 and lived in Oxford for the rest of his life. Mann saw him regularly there. It was one of the very few links with the other life, and it gave him pleasure that his old teacher took an

[2] *Clunet* Pt. 4 page III.

interest in his academic work, particularly his growing preoccupation with public international law. Wolff was never given the proper opportunity to teach in Oxford to which his distinction entitled him. The University Press published a book of his on private international law, but it was allowed to die and Mann was bitterly disappointed that he was not entrusted with the task of carrying it on in a new edition. It was, Mann thought, "a melancholy waste of genius" that Wolff's teaching mission could not flourish in England. But he never forgot the immense debt he owed this "great and lovable man" whose influence had, he said, pervaded his whole life.

In 1930 Mann began his practical legal education by serving six-monthly terms working successively in courts of various levels and in the offices of the public prosecutor and a well-known law firm. At the same time, his examination results that year led Wolff to accept him at once for the doctorate course and to appoint him his own Faculty Assistant. Both were unusual distinctions. As Assistant his duties were to help the Professor to whom he was assigned by marking students' papers, doing some teaching himself, and generally making himself useful. The Assistants had their own common room in the university where they met to discuss legal problems and other questions of the day. Here Mann began his teaching career and wrote his first articles. The very first was written in 1931 on company law for a weekly legal journal (*Juristische Wochenschrift*). It was at this time that he wrote the dissertation for his doctorate. The thesis was on a technical question of company law, the payment for shares in kind. It was dedicated to his father and printed in book form. The doctoral ceremony was a full dress affair. Mann had to defend a number of legal propositions in formal debate. His opponents

were Eduard Wahl, whom he was to meet again after
the war in Berlin, Edgar Bodenheimer who later held a
chair in California, and Rudolf Heinsheimer who, as
Uri Yadin, became Deputy Attorney-General of Israel
and Professor of Law in Jerusalem. The chairman, fully
robed for the occasion, was Eduard Kohlrausch, Rector of
the University. During the same period he spent much
time researching and writing. He met Walter Hallstein
and helped him on a company law project. "Hence", he
afterwards wrote, "my friendship with the first President
of the European Economic Community, which survived
many tribulations."

If he had been able to stay on in Germany there is
no doubt that he would have combined practice and
academic work, as the tradition in Berlin encouraged.
This is clear from a letter he wrote in August 1933 to
the Institute of International Education in New York,
applying for a job as a lecturer or researcher. He claimed
a "fair knowledge of English and American law" and
said that he had already started a book on company law.
"Besides lecturing at a university, I had intended to go
to the Bar and probably I could have achieved both aims
during the following winter..."

Mann was an outstanding and dedicated student.
He was ambitious and cared above everything for the
quality of his work. Even then his attitude to this was
uncompromising. A girl who was his contemporary
at the university first encountered him while he was
Assistant to Martin Wolff. She thought Mann was
severe and marked her papers without much sympathy.
Her impression was that he had his head in the air and
had little time for ordinary mortals. She later became
the wife of Otto Kahn-Freund, one of Mann's closest
friends. She was right even though she was biased, for

she was a socialist egalitarian. But others confirmed her impressions. He was intolerant of anything but the best. Mann was what is called, sometimes disparagingly, an elitist. Like his father, he would never have taken an active part in politics, but he stood on the liberal right. Later in England, he would move further to the right, to a Thatcherite and somewhat simplistic position, much influenced by what he thought of as the disastrous Labour administration of 1945. But not now.

There was another girl in the law faculty at that time. Eleonore Ehrlich was a mathematician and an Assistant to Eduard Kohlrausch, attached to the Institute of Criminal Law. She was a student of the highest ability and was described by one contemporary as *unglaublich gut* (unbelievably good). She had a good reputation as a teaching Assistant and gathered the exceptionally high number of 39 students in the winter term of 1931. One of the very few women Assistants at that time, she was also one of the first to gain a doctorate. Her thesis dated 1931 was written on "The Betrayal of Commercial Secrets according to English and North American Law". The sources included an impressive list of English text books which would have been more familiar to English than German students. Even then she must have been a fluent reader of English, and particularly legal English. Her promise stood at least as high as that of Mann.

Eleonore (or Lore as she was always known) Ehrlich was not often in the common room, but Mann met her sometimes at the house of her cousin, who happened to be one of his closest Geneva friends. In the summer of 1930 she decided to spend six months in New York. To his surprise she came to find him to say goodbye. He was working on his doctoral thesis, but he wisely put the papers away so that they could have dinner together.

She wrote from New York. The correspondence warmed. When she returned in the spring of the next year they knew that they were in love.

She was named after the actress Eleonore Duse. According to the account written by her mother for her grandchildren, Lore was brought up with her younger sister in a charming suburban house in Breslau with a large architect-designed garden and splendid library. She was born in the same year as Francis Mann, a precocious child who "showed already at a very early age an amazing independence of thought." It was to be a lifelong characteristic. She had a profound love for her father and was permanently wounded by his early death when she was still in her teens. According to Mann, her feelings towards her mother, who emigrated to Israel and lived on into her nineties, were more equivocal. He thought that Lore had reacted against the narrow horizons of her mother's fussy bourgeois Jewish outlook, in particular her capacity to make mountains out of molehills. It became an obsession for Lore to "get away". This may have been unfair. Lore's mother was a cultivated woman who taught history of art. When Mann first met Lore in 1929 she was emancipated and Eton-cropped and very attractive indeed. His description of her at the time they met, but recollected much later, was "dashing, full of zest, curiosity, vivacity, *joie de vivre*, ready to laugh, at the same time highly intelligent, critical, willing to argue and challenge, sometimes merely to provoke, amusing but not superficial ..." It is tempting to wonder which among that carillon of attractions seduced him most. She was more forceful and more uncompromising than he was, or wanted to be: a woman of action, as was clear when the time came for them to decide what to do in face of the menace of Hitler.

Werner Flume was a contemporary and knew them

both. He too was an Assistant and saw Mann every day in the common room or in the library. He became one of his closest friends but their friendship was of a sort that seems strange today. They never went out together to have a meal or to go to a concert. They maintained formal relations always – at least until their friendship was renewed after the war. At Flume's 80th birthday celebrations, Mann made a speech. He said that they had known each other for a long time but had always used *Sie* and never *Du*. Until now .... and, he added, from now on as well. It was not quite true but not wholly wrong.

Flume remembered Mann as warm in friendship and feeling, even sentimental, although not impulsive, and controlled in his thinking. Lore, whom he knew less well and only as Mann's girlfriend, was, he thought, very different: cool and clear in her decision, the stronger of the two. And when he resumed the friendship after the war, he did not find them much changed.

III

The Coming of Hitler

Berlin was on edge during the winter of 1932–3. There was a feeling that violence could erupt anywhere. It was just at this time that Mann went to one of Martin Wolff's lectures and an incident occurred:

> In view of the feeling of tension that prevailed a fellow Faculty Assistant and I decided that, unknown to him, we would follow him into the lecture hall and place ourselves to the right and left slightly behind him. He began to lecture to a hall which was overcrowded, so that many students were standing. After a few minutes he stopped and said: "In the seventh row there is a gentleman who thinks fit to read the Berlin Illustrated Weekly, while so many ladies and gentlemen have to stand. I request the gentleman to leave the hall at once." While there was complete silence a young man in Nazi uniform rose and left the hall. When he was gone there was thunderous applause, but Martin Wolff continued as if nothing had happened. My heart stood still during this scene which could so easily have developed into an ugly incident.

As the twenties gave way to the thirties the cancer was spreading through the body of the Weimar Republic. Conditions were ripe for charlatans, gangsters and, above all, demagogues. Germany had hardly recovered from the sickness of inflation when it was struck by the great depression. The retribution of the Treaty of Versailles was everywhere felt and resented. It prevented the country from regaining its manhood. The tribute exacted by the victorious powers in the form of reparations was vengeful and disabling. It was a time for myths and legends. One of the most potent was that of "the stab in the back", the story that the army had been betrayed on the brink of victory in 1918. Scapegoats were needed to feed the myths. A poisonous anti-Semitism was ready at hand, bubbling near the surface. The distinction which Jews had achieved in so many walks of life during Weimar and the contribution they had made to its culture were used as weapons against them. It was they who were everywhere in positions of influence. Like bacilli, the calumny ran, they had infected the state and now lived like vampires on an enfeebled Germany.

As the atmosphere worsened the Berlin streets were defiled by frequent bloody clashes between the Communist red-shirt gangs and brown-shirted Nazis of the *Sturmabteilung* (SA). On 12th July 1932, for example, Count Harry Kessler noted in his diary that "the unbridled, organised Nazi terror has again claimed seventeen dead and nearly two hundred wounded as its victims." It was "a continuous St. Bartholomew's Massacre, day after day, Sunday after Sunday."

How could street violence on this scale be tolerated in a civilised country? Society had been brutalised by the first war and the civil strife which succeeded it. The republic itself was born of something like civil war. Beyond the Rhineland the victor powers did not occupy the country as they did after the second war, and provide, at least temporarily, an effective, stable order. The successive governments of the Weimar Republic had neither the strength of purpose nor the public backing to put down the paramilitary bands which acted as private armies and roamed the streets looking for trouble. Political violence became acceptable, at times even normal. Democratic institutions were correspondingly discredited. Such conditions were ripe for the emergence of a dictator. Then, as the world slump struck Germany, street violence intensified. The last Chancellors of Weimar, from Brüning onwards, ruled more and more by emergency decree. By doing so they subverted democracy and became accomplices to the coming revolution.

There was a lurid twilight between 1929 and January 1933, when Hitler became Chancellor and night fell. The Nazis had won an important victory in the Reichstag elections of September 1930, increasing the number of their seats from 12 to 107. The Party became a force to be reckoned with. Those who had clear eyes were alerted to the danger. Friedrich Mann and Lore Ehrlich were certainly among them. Thomas Mann, their distinguished namesake, saw precisely what was to come unless the middle classes came to their senses.

In the following month the great novelist published a remarkable article under the title "An Appeal to Reason."[3] The election was a storm warning, he said. He urged the cause of the Social Democrats and gave a vivid description of the character of Nazism. Although the picture is familiar enough in hindsight, in 1930 the vision was prophetic. National Socialism, he wrote, was a movement that could take root in a Germany which was bewildered in mind, hungry in body and impoverished in spirit. And for this the victorious powers bore a heavy responsibility. The evil ideology was a blend of the Nordic creed and Germanic romanticism; its language was "a high-flown, wishy-washy jargon full of mystical good feeling, with hyphenated prefixes like race- and

---

[3] Thomas Mann: *Appell an die Vernunft: Berliner Tageblatt* 18 October 1930.

folk-fellowship-". It set up for homage the darkness of the soul, "the holy procreative underworld". In face of such intoxicating barbarism, reason veiled her face. The militant nationalism of Nazism was, he said, less for consumption abroad than at home. Its foreign policy, at least to start with, would seem reasonable. At home hatred was directed at all who could not subscribe to a fanatical love of the Fatherland. "More and more it looks as though the chief goal were the inner purification of the country." How, the novelist asked, was this possible? How could a people, old and ripe and cultured, conform, even after ten thousand purificatory executions, to the wish-image of a primitive, blue-eyed simplicity? The answer came soon enough.

The Party began to attract respectable friends. Some important figures in the military and industrial establishment were sympathetic, believing that advantage lay in an alliance, and credulously misleading themselves that they could control the vulgar little rabble-rouser. Opportunists gathered. Von Papen, in power just before Hitler, urbane and self-satisfied, continued to have himself photographed, Kessler noted in September 1932, and "strongly gives the impression of a German Gramont, the man of 1870 who light-heartedly manoeuvred his country into catastrophe."

Others suffered the different delusions of complacency. They could not or would not see that the Republic was dying and that the real revolution was coming. Thomas Mann described them in his diaries as "the fools who helped to fatten this monster". He knew the hypnosis at the heart of fascism. In his story "Mario and the Magician", written in 1929 and set in fascist Italy, he employed the sinister image of the conjuror who worked by drugging his audience into a state of suggestibility.

Heinrich Brüning, a man of the centre right and the last serious Chancellor before the deluge, was scathing too about the "lazy bourgeoisie". In a radio broadcast during the crucial 1930 election campaign he urged them to go out and vote for the centre parties. But he confided to his diary that he had misread his countrymen. "Germans want to hear precise sharp orders from the government when the situation gets dangerous."[4] It was right but it was too late.

Friedrich Mann and Lore Ehrlich were neither deluded nor complacent. Although they could not imagine the horrors to come, they foresaw the failure of Weimar and the triumph of fascism. Lore came back from New York in the spring of 1931 determined to cross the Atlantic again as soon as she had qualified. In the summer of the following year Mann had an offer from a firm of Munich lawyers (Professor Rheinstrom and Dr. Alfred Werner) to join them as a partner after he had qualified. It had not been his intention to leave Berlin, but conditions were worsening in the capital and friends urged on him the attractions of Munich and the reputation of Rheinstrom and Werner. He decided to see for himself and work for a while in the firm's office. So on 28 February 1933 he took the night train to Munich. It was a fateful night and, for Mann, a fateful step. As the train pulled out of the station the sky was red from the Reichstag fire.

He started work in Munich the next day, but it was not long before he knew that it was not for him. The practice was ordinary and the atmosphere was provincial. There was another bad sign. He had been brought up by his father to understand that the giving of free legal advice

---

[4] Heinrich Brüning: *Memoiren 1918–1934*. Deutsche Verlags-Anstalt. Stuttgart 1970, page 185.

for those who could not afford to pay was an absolute professional obligation (there then being no state-funded scheme), and that such cases called for extra care. The Rheinstrom firm neither accepted nor practised that convention. Rheinstrom, however, had friends in London. One of them was Sir Albert Bennett, a Conservative MP and industrialist, whose son-in-law Douglas Phillips was a solicitor and a partner in the firm of Swann, Hardman of Norfolk Street, just off The Strand. Within days of Mann arriving in Munich, Rheinstrom left for London on business. For all the shortcomings of his practice Rheinstrom proved to be a good friend. Mann kept in touch with him and when, during the war, Rheinstrom was living and working in New York and the Manns' two small children, David and Jessica, were in North America, he took an interest in their welfare and did all he could to find a good home for them.

Meanwhile, with Hitler's coming to power at the end of January, life for Jews in Berlin – and throughout Germany – was becoming less bearable day by day and more precarious at each moment. None knew when he might lose his job or be offered insult or violence in the street by the stormtroopers who roamed unchecked.

Hitler's objectives had been clear since soon after the first world war. The humiliation and chaos of Germany must be redeemed by restoring national pride and making her the most powerful nation in Europe. She would expand eastwards, Communism would be rooted out, and the Jews who everywhere from Wall Street to Bolshevik Moscow had been enemies of the state were to be removed. All this could be read in *Mein Kampf* (1925–6) or gathered from his speeches. The themes never varied as he approached nearer to the seat of power. The failures and ultimate suicide of the Weimar Republic served only to strengthen the cogency of what he was preaching.   His programme of national redemption, prosperity, unity, manhood proved irresistible to the German people. To understand this is to go some way to explain the seemingly inexplicable – how a nonentity whose aims were perversions could attain dictatorial powers and, eventually, heroic stature.

With his appointment as Chancellor on 30 January 1933, Hitler could at last harness his own malign charisma to the machinery of a modern state. He moved quickly. On 28 February, the day after the Reichstag fire and in the chaos of the consequent anti-communist hysteria, he was given emergency powers by President Hindenburg. Immediately after the elections in March, when the Nazis and their allies gained an overall majority, the Reichstag voted itself out of existence by granting Hitler the means to full executive and legislative authority. The revolution was swiftly accomplished, and formally in accordance with law.

In January 1933 there were half a million Jews living in Germany, emancipated and hardly discriminated against. They were now to be "cleansed" from the community. It could not happen all at once if only because Jews occupied so many crucial positions in the professions, in commerce and industry, and in the arts. But step by step it was to be done. This is not to say that state-sponsored mass murder was already planned: it came gradually by its own black logic to become actual policy as part of the invasion of Russia eight years later. Nevertheless, the notion of a "pure" German race had been at the centre of Hitler's thinking since the early twenties.

The first moves were made in the arts, that most visible manifestation of the free mind and where Jews were particularly prominent.   Otto Klemperer and

Bruno Walter were forced to leave Germany within weeks of Hitler coming to power. Walter was informed through rumours put abroad by Goebbels' Propaganda Ministry that the Philharmonic Hall would be burned down if he went ahead with a concert at which he was to conduct the Berlin Philharmonic Orchestra. The incident was instructive and would probably have been known by Mann. Richard Strauss took Walter's place. As a consequence Toscanini refused to conduct at the Bayreuth festival that summer.[5]

In April, "non-Aryans" (a closely defined term) were excluded from the civil service which included both academic and judicial office. A notice dated 19 April disqualifying Mann survives. Within days discrimination against Jewish lawyers and doctors was formalised. Nazism penetrated the universities. They were an early target because the traditional spirit of free enquiry might crystallise into a nucleus of dissent. Notorious Nazis like Carl Schmitt, the tame jurist of the Party, were "implanted" as Professors by order of the Ministry. An association of Nazi students was formed and quickly made a nuisance of itself. The members could not be disciplined in the normal way. In April the Director of Administration in the University required each Assistant to make a declaration that he or she was of "Aryan" descent and would give unquestioning allegiance to the state. Any who could not or did not were liable to be dismissed. In February, Mann had withdrawn his application for re-appointment as an Assistant and asked for a term's leave of absence. He did not make the declaration required by the Director of Administration. He knew what was coming.

---

[5] Saul Friedlander: *Nazi Germany and the Jews. The Years of Persecution 1933–39*, page 9.

The story of the law faculty of the *Friedrich-Wilhelms-Universität* (Berlin University) in the revolution of 1933 has now been told in well-documented detail in *The Naked Spirit* by Anna-Maria Gräfin von Lösch.[6] It is a human story of how both teacher and student were called on to face the most severe crisis of conscience; and it is vividly illustrated by tracing the career of one or two individuals whose lives crossed Mann's during that time.

Eduard Kohlrausch was Rector of the University, Director of its Institute of Criminology and Lore Ehrlich's Professor. He was of course well known to Mann, who was to encounter him again in the immediate aftermath of the collapse of Hitler's Reich. He had first been appointed a Professor in 1919 and became Rector in 1932. In his inaugural address he encouraged the students to gain an understanding of the political life of the country.[7] When Hitler came to power in the following year he tried to do his best. On 1 April 1933, when uniformed men of the SA locked up some Jewish students and took over a room in the University buildings, Kohlrausch ordered them to release the captives and get out. They did. He was told that all institutions of higher learning would be subordinated as from 11 March not only to the Education Ministry, but also to Goebbels' newly formed Propaganda Ministry. He must have known what that would mean. Kohlrausch was not anti-Semitic, but he felt increasingly that he had to conform. At the beginning of April he reported to Rust, the Education Minister, that he had talked to an unruly group of 100 or more students who were making a noise about Martin Wolff. He reminded them that many of them liked and revered him. Some

---

[6] Tubingen 1999.
[7] Lösch: pages 113–114.

had agreed but said it was for the sake of a higher cause. He had agreed with them, he reported, and told them "to lead the battle for de-Semitisation by fair means and within the limits laid down by the Ministry."[8] He was beginning to speak the language of Orwell but he was still willing to make a stand. On 10 May there was a burning of books in front of the University with Goebbels present. Kohlrausch wrote to Hitler and to Rust to protest. A few days earlier Martin Wolff's classes had been disrupted by student rowdies. Kohlrausch was the only staff member to intervene and help him.[9] His equivocal record must have been noticed by the authorities and he was replaced as Rector later in the month. He continued to trim his sails under the stress of events and survived in Berlin University throughout the Third Reich. Mann probably knew the full story and did not condemn him. Both the Manns were moved and distressed when they had news of Kohlrausch's death.

Werner Flume was Mann's close friend. In 1932 he came to Berlin from Bonn as Fritz Schulz's Assistant, having already been awarded his doctorate. Schulz was a distinguished Roman lawyer and legal historian whom Mann much admired, and Flume wished to complete his studies with him in Berlin so that he could take the final examination that would qualify him for a university teaching post. But these plans were frustrated because Schulz was half Jewish and was told in September 1933 that he would have to leave Berlin. In the event Flume failed his final examination later in the same year, as did three other Assistants of equally marked ability.[10] It

---

[8] Lösch: page 173.

[9] Lösch: pages 128, 132, 135.

[10] Lösch: page 226.

seems clear that these results were attributable to political reasons, certainly in Flume's case. In March 1933 an Assistant called Gerd Voss, who also held a position in the SA with the title of Students' *Sturmführer*, had called all the Assistants together and demanded a boycott of the Jewish Professors. Voss had been Martin Wolff's Assistant since 1931. Flume flared up and told Voss precisely what he would think of him if he boycotted Wolff whom, as Flume knew, Voss personally admired. Voss threatened him with the "SA cellar", a notorious place for beatings. Nothing of the sort happened, but Voss reported the incident to the Dean and told him that Flume was politically undesirable. The Dean advised Flume to complete his final qualification elsewhere.[11]

Flume considered himself fortunate that fate had spared him the terrible dilemma he would have had to face if he, like Kohlrausch, had remained in academic life. Instead he took a quiet job as an internal lawyer with a publishing house and was not able to complete his qualification for a Professorial Chair until Hitler had gone. In 1948 Mann met him in Düsseldorf for the first time since his marriage fifteen years earlier when Flume had acted as witness. That was the day Mann had left Germany for good and Flume did not then know whether he would ever see his friend again. The years of darkness intervened. Flume had steadfastly refused to join the Nazi Party during the Hitler years. Mann had nothing but admiration for the integrity of his friend who had stood by his principles when so many had given way. They saw each other regularly in their new post-war lives.

---

[11] Lösch: page 232 and author's interview with Flume. Voss had spoken of Wolff as having "opened up his mind to the beauty of the law" (Lösch: page 177). In 1934 Voss was killed in the *Putsch* against Röhm which destroyed the SA.

The reaction of the Jews themselves to Hitler's accession to power was uncertain. Some understood that jealousy was swelling the tide of anti-Semitism and were anxious not to provoke the Nazis into more extreme measures. They began to look for ways of appeasing the regime. Some even felt sympathy with the idea that Jews were too prominent in certain fields. Thomas Mann, who was not a Jew but was married to one, certainly thought so. "It is no calamity after all that the domination of the legal system by the Jews has been ended", he wrote in his diary on 9 April 1933.[12] Martin Wolff was among those who deluded themselves that there were ways in which the Jews of Germany could help themselves. In 1933 he was one of five Professors of Jewish descent out of a total of fourteen; but he was as naive as great scholars can sometimes be. He thought it possible to make sacrifices to placate the monster. It seems that he proposed at a faculty meeting that all Jewish Assistants should be dismissed.[13] According to a contemporary, he disapproved of those Jewish parvenus who by their behaviour were pushing public opinion further into anti-Semitism, so that "the other more distinguished Jews, those who were 'Germanised' (*eingedeutscht*), had a difficult time making themselves felt".[14] A snobbery perhaps, but it was fanciful to suppose that the Nazis would interest themselves in such distinctions. He and those who thought like him did not understand the nature of the events which were engulfing Germany at frightening speed. His own fate was inevitable. In 1935

[12] Thomas Mann: *Tagebücher 1933–34* ed. Mendelssohn. Frankfurt-am-Main 1977 page 46.
[13] Lösch: page 152.
[14] Lösch: page 175.

he lost his post at the University and in 1938 he applied for and obtained permission to emigrate to England, his wife being British.

Richard Mann and his sister-in-law also left Germany in 1938 and settled in Oxford. He died there in 1953. He had ceased to practise law in Germany in 1934 as a result of a case he had in the appeal court for a Jewish client accused of a breach of the recently enacted exchange control regulations. Shortly before the hearing of the appeal one of the judges told him that he and his colleagues had read the papers in the case and that, although his client ought to be acquitted, they would have to convict because he was Jewish. The judge confessed that there had been such an outburst in the Nazi press against him and his family about another recent acquittal of a Jew, he could not take the risks involved in the acquittal of a second Jew. Richard Mann immediately had his name removed from the roll of practising advocates.

Friedrich and Lore Mann who had seen it all coming, would have thought it futile to suppose that there was anything the Jews themselves could do to avert the storm. Mann made this clear long afterwards. In 1968 he reviewed a book called *Letters to a young German*.[15] The author, Heinrich Kronstein, was a German Jewish lawyer who had emigrated to the United States. Included in the book was the text of a letter that he had written in 1932 to Carl Schmitt, the Nazi legal theorist and anti-Semite. He was the same Schmitt who acquired a chair in Berlin by favour of the Party, and who in 1934, after the brutal murder of Röhm, the leader of the SA, published an article entitled "The Führer protects the Law".[16] In his letter

---

[15] *Politisches Buch*. 29 March 1968. No. 13. *Memoirs of a Lawyer*.
[16] Ian Kershaw: *Hitler: 1889–1936: Hubris* page 521.

Kronstein recommended to Schmitt that for a planned society the comparatively small population of German Jews should be spread more thinly through the broader German community. "The unavoidable sacrifices", he wrote, "which individual Jews might have to make would surely be gladly accepted by them if it were thereby made possible for them to remain part of the German people."

Mann treated the entire memoir harshly and this particular suggestion to a dose of heavy sarcasm. It was surprising, he said, that Schmitt had never thought to reply to these suggestions. One would have expected him to send Mr. Kronstein to East Prussia to be a swineherd so as to further the interests of the sacrifice-loving minority. He was never at his best when he was really angry.

In early 1933 Munich was no safer than Berlin. In March, when Thomas Mann had just begun his self-exile to Switzerland, his daughter brought "innumerable stories of idiocies and atrocities from Munich, arrests, brutal treatment etc., which add to our perturbation and disgust ... ". Then, at the end of the month, the diary recorded that in Breslau all Jews had had their passports revoked, while in Munich there was a systematic boycott of all Jewish-owned businesses.

All this occurred during Mann's first weeks in Munich. He met Lore for a week-end to discuss what they should do. She had no doubt that they should emigrate at once. At the beginning of April all Jews were excluded from the Bar. Lore had been manhandled and thrown out of court by thugs in SA uniform. That was enough for her. But he was unable to decide so quickly and wanted to talk things over with his father. On his way to Frankenthal he stopped to see an old family friend in Heidelberg, Karl Geiler. He was a distinguished commercial lawyer and, as it happened, he had edited Mann's dissertation for his doctorate and written a laudatory foreword. Geiler put his arm round the young man's shoulder. "But my dear Mann, why don't you take shelter in my office while this thunderstorm lasts?" Typically ostrich-like was Mann's comment. But the misjudgement, however gross, was common enough. Geiler lived on through the thunderstorm and held his chair at Heidelberg until 1939 when his licence was withdrawn. Then, after the war, the American military administration asked him to form a civil government in Hesse where he became its first prime minister in 1945. His reputation was clean.

That all lay in the future. For the present, Rheinstrom now sent a message from London asking Mann to come to see him there. It had become clear that it would be impossible for Rheinstrom to return to Munich and he wanted to discuss a plan he had devised. Mann went to London in April to meet him. The idea was that Rheinstrom and Werner would emigrate to France and open an office in Paris for German lawyers to practise German law. Mann was to do the same in London, working closely with Swann, Hardman from a room in Norfolk Street. Implausible though it was, the German Ambassador in London, whom Rheinstrom knew, had obtained permission for this arrangement from the British Home Secretary. After returning briefly to Berlin to tidy up his affairs and to discuss the extraordinary turn of events with Lore, Mann was back in London in May, living miserably in a cheap and nasty hotel and suffering in freakishly hot weather from hay fever. He must have been suffering at least as much from an acute sense of dislocation and loss.

While he was there he received fresh evidence of the unpredictable ways of bureaucracy. Lore telephoned to say that an official from the Berlin Court of Appeal had rung her to ask whether she was not friendly with Dr. Mann. She had no notion how he knew, but she had answered yes, but he was abroad. Please tell him then that, although he has been dismissed from legal service, as a result of a new regulation he will now be able to take his final examination and obtain his qualification: it would be a pity if he did not avail himself of the opportunity.

So he returned one last time to Berlin, but without enthusiasm for the qualification he was there to complete. In his mind he had already turned away from Germany. He had to prepare himself for a new life in a strange country, whatever it might bring. Even then, with his prospect in ruins, he was probably clear-headed enough to know that the country of his birth could never be the same again. And if he saw it, Lore saw it at least as clearly. Both of them sat their examinations in October, Lore with distinction, he without – not that he cared, he remarked bitterly.

They were married the day after her examination, planning to leave for good on a morning train. They pressed the registrar to carry out the civil ceremony early so that they would not miss the train. That official looked the bride up and down insolently and asked: Is it so urgent? There, under the ubiquitous picture of Hitler, they were joined in the presence of two of their university friends, Erika Kempf and Werner Flume. It was the last service his corrupted country did him. There were no celebrations. There was no time and in any case it would hardly have been appropriate.

Francis Mann insisted that there was nothing heroic about their decision to leave Germany. It was prosaic and obvious. If they were to survive they had to go. But, as he wrote in his unpublished memoir, others faced an appalling dilemma.

The point which has pursued me all my life is an entirely different one: can I (or anyone in my position) who was free from any present or prospective persecution, and who had complete freedom of choice and who could move in either direction honestly say of himself that he would not have joined the new regime? He might not have participated in, but might have excused the worst excesses. He might not have been a member of the Party, but preferred to be a sympathiser. Who has the right to criticise others if he has not himself positively proved that he would have behaved differently, that he would not have been a Party member or sympathiser, that he would have had the moral courage to act independently, according to his conscience, his faith, according to the laws of morality?

He and his wife left because they were Jews. "We were not, we are not, practising Jews. But we felt as Jews by background, history and tradition, even though our noses are straight and our cultural status was wholly and firmly German. We did not emigrate on account of political persecution, because we were not politicians." It was characteristically straightforward of him that he would not claim the false credit of having the virtue of the dissenter of conscience.

IV

London

The Manns travelled to Paris and arrived on the morning
of Friday 13 October, 1933.   They stayed with their
friends the Thannhausers at the Hotel Regina before going
on to London on the Monday. The week-end passed for
a honeymoon and they now faced the unknown. They
had no money other than 10 marks each in notes and a
return railway ticket which could be cashed. They had
earlier smuggled some bank notes to friends in England
by pasting them into Nazi propaganda leaflets. Their first
home was a boarding house in Golders Green, but they
quickly found a cheap furnished flat near the Edgware
Road which could be had for £6 a month.

It is impossible to do more than guess what were the
emotions of the newly married couple at this moment.
They had lost everything: possessions, life, prospect.
They had just passed through a nightmare which would
always be there in memory. If they did look back, they
never talked about it to others. But now in the winter
of 1933 they were in an alien land with qualifications
and experience that were of little value. Even their safety
could not be guaranteed. Permission to stay was open to
review each year, and even if it were to prove possible to
settle here, there could be no hope for them if England
were overrun and lost the coming war. So much the
worse if the craven government in Westminster were to
make an accommodation with Hitler.

The hopes and fears, preconceptions and prejudices, taboos and attitudes of the Britain the Manns first saw were to be changed almost out of recognition by the second world war. The working man and his family lived then under the threat of a week's notice to quit their home, and a week's notice of dismissal from employment without compensation. Unemployment was at record levels. Society was monochrome in race, skin pigment and, at least formal, adherence to the Anglican order. Men wore hats and raised them on the top of the bus as they passed the Cenotaph in Whitehall. In the collective memory was the fear of war and its ravages. There was the also the fear of poverty and hunger, without any safety net supplied by the state, that the slump had marked on men's minds. The telegrams telling of the death of young men in Flanders and the march from Jarrow were part of the national consciousness.

Although the officials at the Home Office who were processing the refugees' applications to enter Britain did their work fairly and humanely, the social welcome was cool. The climate was insular and anti-Semitism was widespread. The prejudice was polite, submerged and would hardly have been admitted by those who gave it house room in their minds. Neville Chamberlain's attitude was probably representative of the ruling caste. He thought anti-Semitism was caused more by envy than anything else and he was genuinely appalled by the violence against Jews in Germany; and not only because it threatened his object of achieving European peace by appeasing Hitler. But in a letter to his sister, Hilda, six years on (30 July 1939)[17] about the stories of atrocities

---

[17] Neville Chamberlain papers. Cadbury Research Library, Birmingham: NC/18/1/1110; Robert Self: *The Neville Chamberlain Diary Letters*, vol. 4, page 433.

that were then at last being given credence in England, he revealed his instinctive feelings: "No doubt Jews aren't a loveable people; I don't care about them myself – but that is not sufficient to explain the pogrom."

The Manns did not lament their fate. They would have thought it a waste of time. They despised self-pity and they were always quick to detect anything done or said with the intention of gratifying feelings. It is their courage and resolution that compels admiration. They simply made the best of it and set to energetically to make a life and career in their new home. First they had to establish an office in the room that had been set aside at 10 Norfolk Street. They did not know whether any clients would appear but they went out to buy some Woolworths fittings. A carpet and a book case each cost them £2. They had brought a typewriter from Germany. Their expenses were minimal. Even so, it is hard to see how they actually survived. The first receipt from the office (two guineas from a firm of solicitors) was not recorded until January 1934 and they were not able to take anything out of the practice until July of that year. Richard Mann must have been able to help them in this first tentative period.

The earliest Jewish refugees formed a close community, often doing jobs for which they were not trained and providing each other with most of their needs. The enclave was in the north-west suburbs – Hampstead, Maida Vale, Golders Green – where many of them or their families still are. So it was natural that Mann's first clients would be refugees themselves, needing advice on German law. Later, as Nazism spread eastwards, the practice began to include clients from Austria and the other countries bordering the Reich to the east. The problems were concerned with entry and work permits, leases or forming small businesses. Mann also recalled an unpleasant line of cases from these days. Someone would succeed, at risk to himself for breaching the tyrannous laws in force in Germany, in smuggling out money or valuables owned by an acquaintance who was already in England. He then refused to hand them over. Could the stolen property be recovered in English courts? Mann thought the point a delicate one. But in his experience it was never decided because he always advised, with bitterness in his heart, in favour of a compromise.

The Manns were never free of anxiety about the security of their status as, in his own disarming words, they were "guests enjoying hospitality" with permits to stay only for a year at a time. Refugees were granted permission to enter on the simple undertaking of the Jewish Refugee Committee that they would not be a charge on the public purse. It remained so until 1938 when a visa system had to be introduced to cope with a flood of desperate people following the annexation of Austria, the Munich crisis and, in November, *Kristallnacht*, the night of broken glass when, after the destruction of shops and businesses, many thousands of Jews were rounded up and taken to the concentration camps. Lore never applied for a work permit in Britain. She knew that only one of an immigrant couple could get a permit and that if she applied for one, she would probably jeopardise her husband's situation. This prevented her until a late stage in her life from having the professional career to which her own ability and academic record so clearly entitled her. Their anxiety may have been misplaced and it certainly caused resentment in her, but they could not afford to take chances when life and livelihood were at stake.

There has been some harsh criticism of British immigration policy during the thirties. In view of the fate that met those who were left behind in Germany, Austria and the countries of eastern Europe, it is almost impossible to avoid hindsight in trying to make a judgement. To those who are critical, it was a weak and illiberal British government and an equally weak, and apologetic, Anglo-Jewish leadership who together contrived to shut the door on many who sought refuge from certain death. Mann himself did not think so. His judgement was that the Home Secretary and his officials exercised their discretion reasonably and sympathetically. Joan Stiebel, who worked as the only Gentile for the remarkable Otto Schiff[18] and his refugees' committee from 1933 onwards, agreed. She found the Home Office very understanding at a time when it was under great pressure. Britain then was not an immigration country, and there was genuine apprehension that a large influx of Jewish refugees might provoke an outburst of anti-Jewish feeling. At a time of high unemployment the last thing the man in the street wanted was the arrival of large numbers of destitute people looking for work.

The point about anti-Semitism was one which was naturally felt by Mann. He and his wife found it difficult to make friends with some members of the Jewish

[18] Otto Moritz Schiff: born Frankfurt-am-Main 1875, member of a well-known Jewish family. He came to England as a young man and worked on the Stock Exchange. In the early years of the 20th century he helped Jewish refugees from Russia and Poland in the Temporary Shelter in Mansell Street in the East End. On the outbreak of war in 1914 the Shelter was temporary home to refugees from Belgium, including 12,000 Jews, who were repatriated with his help at the end of the war. In 1933 a new influx of refugees from Germany needed help with resettlement. Schiff played the leading role. He earned the trust of the Home Office and many decisions were taken on little more than his recommendation. Chairman of the German-Jewish Aid Committee. Awarded the O.B.E. for his work with Belgian refugees and the C.B.E. for his later work with German refugees. Died 1952.

community who were already well established in Britain. Neville Laski, a well-known King's Counsel,[19] advised him over tea one day that a career in the law was a hopeless quest and that he should think of chicken farming. Mann was not inclined either to take or forget patronising advice. The truth was that those who had achieved assimilation did not always welcome new entrants. People like the Manns presented no threat to those who were already here, but they were still not welcomed with open arms.

While Mann was impressed by the way in which the Home Office dealt with fugitives from Germany, he was maddened by the complacency and blindness with which the government and the ruling classes faced the rising menace of its evil genius. He found both Conservatives and Labour Party members anxious to conciliate Hitler, deluding themselves that it was possible to do business with him. He perceived the policy of appeasement as no more than an excuse for moral cowardice. He had seen it all before in the crumbling degeneration of the Weimar Republic, and that made it the more intolerable. But he knew that as a guest in the country, with relatives still in Germany and liable to reprisals, he could not speak out.

Little by little the Manns' situation improved. By October 1935 he was able to tell the Home Office that the gross earnings of the London office of Rheinstrom, Werner

[19] Neville Laski, then President of the London Committee of Deputies of British Jews, led a group of representatives of the Jewish Community to the Home Office in April 1933. They proposed that all Jewish refugees from Germany should be admitted without distinction, and formally undertook that "all expense, whether in respect of temporary or permanent accommodation or maintenance will be borne by the Jewish community without ultimate charge to the State". The other representatives who signed the undertaking were Lionel Cohen (later Lord Cohen, the Law Lord), L.G. Montefiore, and Otto Schiff.

and Mann for the latest year were "more than £500" and that the clients included Alfred Dunhill, and a number of well-known London firms of solicitors. Richard Mann and Lore's mother were able to send some money, and even furniture and pictures. The Manns moved first to a better flat near Regent's Park in 1934, and then in 1936 to a good house in Clifton Hill, St. John's Wood. Their first child, Esther, was stillborn in 1934, David was born in September 1935 and Jessica in September 1937.

In 1935, while Lore was pregnant, they visited Palestine to see Lore's sister, Eva. She had gone there in 1934 and was urging them to join her. They wanted to see if it might be a place to settle instead of England. Lore liked the simplicity and sunshine of the life but it came to nothing. There was a story, possibly apocryphal, that he could not bear the dirty fingernails which he saw everywhere. Whether or not Lore was a Zionist then, she could have felt more at home in the life of a *kibbutz* than in the English social scene. Her husband felt differently. He would not have been willing to give up European life and culture, particularly the country which had given him shelter. Mann was certainly not a Zionist. He did not believe that the choice for Jews was either to assimilate and ultimately lose their identity, or to go to live in Israel. He was not bothered by divided loyalties or the tension in the mind of the assimilated Jew between Jewishness and Englishness. He considered that it was perfectly possible to live as a citizen of a European country and still preserve a distinctive Jewish culture which would contribute to the life of the nation. Why not? His family had done it in Germany for centuries.

Meanwhile he wrestled with the problem of whether to qualify as a barrister or a solicitor. His first love was the academic life. It had an attraction that nothing else had.

Only there was the satisfaction and the true freedom. He explained it in a revealing letter to his wife written in 1946. "I believe I have a pronounced *akademische Dünkel* (academic pride or arrogance) and au fond I believe I feel that work other than academic is not really worthwhile and that it is the academic spirit which separates us from Bokanovsky ... and all the other attractions of the Brave New World."[20] Mann never changed his mind about the importance of freedom of thought as a defence against the nightmare prophesies of Huxley and Orwell. And he never ceased to regret that he was unable to obtain an academic post in England – as he did in Germany.

In the choice between the two sides of the profession, solicitors and the Bar, the latter would have more easily allowed him to pursue his academic interests. But there were difficulties which appeared insuperable. He now had a young family and at any time he might have to support his father, his aunt and Lore's mother if, as he felt sure, they would all be forced to leave Germany. The most pressing thing for him was to have a reliable income, and a new barrister's income was unpredictable. He also thought that his pronounced German accent would be a disadvantage for a barrister. Would solicitors send work to, or would judges accept, someone who did not have an English voice? This was after all a time when Germany was perceived as an enemy and war was more than a possibility.

So, with regret, he decided to become a solicitor. Regret because to his mind it was to choose second best. At that time solicitors did not undertake serious legal research

[20] Bokanovsky's Process: in Aldous Huxley's *Brave New World*, a process of fertilising eggs in a system of human genetic manipulation. Mann was reading the book at the time. It made a deep impression on him.

and could not argue cases in court. There were some 20,000 solicitors compared with a specialist Bar of 2000. The Bar was an elite and membership conferred a social superiority over the solicitors' branch which in any case was of uneven quality. These were considerations that would certainly have weighed with Mann.

He was a student of the *mores* of the divided English legal profession, some of which were bizarre and defied all logic. As an outsider he could have written a good book about it. But he was never tempted to stray beyond the bounds of academic writing, and what he did was by example. Much has been done to improve the relative standing of solicitors since pre-war days, and the profession owes a lot to a handful of outstanding practitioners, among whom Mann was pre-eminent.

He would have to become a British subject by naturalisation before he could practise as a solicitor and it was not until 1938, when he had completed five years' residence in England, that this became a possibility. At that point Henry Hardman, senior partner of Swann, Hardman, the Norfolk Street firm which had provided Mann with a room in his earliest days in England, agreed to give him articles. The active partner in the firm was now Douglas Phillips, a type of Englishman that Mann admired. A man of upright bearing and generous character without a trace of prejudice of any sort, his friendship from the start had been the greatest support to Mann. Phillips' essential "Englishness" and his background of Oxford and the Guards provided Mann, when they became partners after the war, with a dimension and a solidity which he needed. Of the many kindnesses he did, the introduction to John Foster, an Oxford friend of Phillips and an influential and well-connected member of the Bar, was probably the most important. Foster was a most unusual character, a lifelong bachelor with a vast circle of friends.   Miriam Rothschild, one of the closest of these, described him in her essay in the Dictionary of National Biography as first and foremost a true egalitarian.   "He possessed a rare combination of ebullience, cleverness, good humour, delight in the kaleidoscope of human affairs, an unselfish and practical interest in the successes and tribulations of friends and acquaintances, and the gift of combining a crystal-clear objectivity with great kindness and an infinite capacity for helping those in trouble."[21] He had many friends in the Jewish community and worked tirelessly for their welfare.   He and Mann took greatly to each other and Foster sent him a steady stream of valuable work.

In 1938 Douglas Phillips went to Germany to see what could be done for those of Lore's family who were still trapped there.   It had become difficult and dangerous to try to keep in touch by post with the German Jews who remained in Germany; and this was a journey with some serious risk to Phillips himself.   The Czech crisis was at its height.   Richard Mann and his sister-in-law had left earlier that year.   Many Jews were being taken into concentration camps and could be released only on proof that they would emigrate immediately. Visas were essential and in their desperation Jews were seeking them for many obscure destinations – Ceylon, China, Costa Rica.   Phillips went to Breslau, the home of Lore's family, and visited the British and American Consulates in Berlin.   While he was still in the capital, the London office took a telephone call from a reputable firm of London solicitors seeking an urgent interview

---

[21] *Dictionary of National Biography*, 1981–85, Oxford University Press 1990, page 145.

with Hardman, the senior partner in Norfolk Street. A meeting followed. The solicitor told Hardman that he had been informed by the department in the Foreign Office concerned with political intelligence that Phillips was in danger and should return to London immediately. Phillips interrupted his errand of mercy and came home, and within a day or so, his relieved wife and the Manns met him at Victoria Station. The mystery of how the Foreign Office knew about the visit, and why the warning was given and communicated in this strange way was never explained.

Mann became an employee of an office consisting only of Hardman, Douglas Phillips and two managing clerks. He remembered the atmosphere as being the friendliest. Mann's secretary, Dori Furth, herself a refugee who afterwards went to live in New York, also had a happy memory of that office. It compared most favourably with her experience in New York. Her office then, she told the Manns in a letter written in March 1942, was a noisy place with much shouting from "the rougher type of male Brooklyn voices". "Never forget that this is not 10 Norfolk Street... As for our clients, most of them are, to say the least, sickening. Compared with them, the visitors at 10 Norfolk Street were *la crème de la crème*." It was in that civilised London environment that Mann embarked on his English professional career.

The coming of war in September 1939 changed everything. It was an unhappy chance for the Manns that they were not naturalised in time. They had applied at the first possible moment in September 1938 and later discovered that their papers were ready for signature when the halt was called. They were not granted naturalisation until 1946, and in the meantime they became "enemy aliens" instead. During the first winter of the war and while they were living in a furnished cottage in Surrey, the internment of aliens under the notorious Defence Regulation 18B was brought into force. Many Jews and others who had the greatest imaginable incentive to help Britain in its struggle were detained without trial or proper investigation. "An insane policy" was Mann's description.   They were interviewed by police who apparently shared his view, for they steadfastly refused to do anything at all about interning the Manns. They played for time, they found pretexts, they pursued a tactic of masterly inactivity – until detention orders tailed off at the end of 1940.

War brought more frustration. This was a war which both of them had seen coming since 1933. All this time England slept. Now, listening to Neville Chamberlain announcing Britain's declaration of war on the radio, they heard a defeated and an almost apologetic tone. The war, Mann felt keenly, was his and his people's war; but he was not going to be able to fight, and it seemed that it would not be fought with the resolution that was going to be indispensable.

The morning after Chamberlain's broadcast Douglas Phillips drove them back to London from Oxford, where Richard Mann and his sister-in-law were living. Phillips told them on the way that Mann would now have to drop the "Fritz" by which he was usually called, and adopt some other name. But what?   Lore expressed her dislike of "Frederick" or "Fred", and so they hit upon "Francis", the name which now seems inseparable from the man. Nevertheless, when in 1947 he changed his name formally by deed poll, he took the names "Frederick Alexander".

Their worst fears were realised in the early months of the war. The Germans swept all before them and the Chamberlain government that through the thirties had so palpably failed to recognise the true nature of the peril facing Britain, was now fighting a war with no better show of determination or realism. Churchill, the "single, unforgettable voice" of warning, in Mann's phrase, came to power in May 1940, but was it already too late? Although no one knew it then, Churchill was fighting his own battle in the War Cabinet against a faction led by Halifax that wanted to open negotiations through Mussolini to take Britain out of the war.[22] Mann would not have been surprised. Halifax epitomised that mixture of *hauteur* and unwillingness to face facts which so maddened him. But he and Lore now had to think again of survival. They decided to send their two children to North America where friends offered to look after them.

David and Jessica left in the summer of 1940. David was 4 and Jessica 2. They were not sent away to escape the bombing. The Manns had no thought that the children should be spared what everyone else in Britain had to face. But they were convinced that England would be invaded and occupied, and that Jews would suffer a dreadful fate. Their first thought was to save their children – not themselves. The two small children went first to friends in Canada. The wife had been a favourite pupil of Laura Oppenheim, when she was teaching in Tunbridge Wells and before she went home to Germany to keep house for Richard Mann. They had kept in touch. But, after about a

---

[22] On 26 May 1940, the day before the evacuation of British forces from Dunkirk started, Halifax produced a memorandum for the War Cabinet headed "Suggested Approach to Signor Mussolini." It said: "If Signor Mussolini will co-operate with us in securing a settlement of all European questions which safeguard[s] the independence and security of the Allies, and could be the basis of a just and durable peace for Europe, we will undertake at once to discuss...." See John Lukacs: *Five Days in London. May 1940*: page 118.

year, it became impossible for them to stay on because of the illness of their hosts, and the children went down to the United States to live with their great aunt (on Francis' side) in Connecticut, a widow without children of her own. Of course Francis and Lore Mann were worried about their children's welfare, and they brought them home as soon as they could after the threat of invasion had gone. In the height and stress of war with U-boats prowling in the Atlantic, getting a berth on a vessel sailing east was almost an impossibility. But somehow it was arranged and the two children returned circuitously in the summer of 1943 by ship to Lisbon, then flying boat to Ireland, and finally by ferry across the Irish Sea.

The experiences of those children who crossed the Atlantic in wartime were mixed. Mann's daughter Jessica wrote a vivid account of it in her book, *Out of Harm's Way: The Wartime Evacuation of Children from Britain* (2005). Some had an exciting time and revelled in the adventure. But for the more sensitive children, the loss of parents without the certainty that the family would ever be re-united, was something which could have incalculable consequences. The anxieties of parents who knew the perils cannot have been less. The evacuation got a mixed press. Jessica recalled that the American media described the children as the Young Ambassadors, and American and Canadian families were ready to give the evacuees the warmest welcome. But some English newspapers called them the "Gone with the Wind-ups". The Headmaster of Winchester thought it was his duty, without any knowledge of individual circumstances, to write to *The Times* to say that children should not be encouraged to think of their own safety first. Some parents received white feathers through the post. To read all this now is to cast a strange backward light on the attitudes then prevailing in Britain. Above all, there was no general recognition in 1940 of the peculiar horrors that threatened the children of Jewish families.

Francis Mann wanted to fight, but in the end he gave up the attempt to join the armed forces and yielded to Douglas Phillips' entreaty that he stay to look after the practice while Phillips was away in the war. "I did what I could to help my dear friend and tried to keep the nest warm for him." Lore was also unable to join the forces and became a supervisor with a company manufacturing light bulbs. With the children gone, they moved back to London with week-ends in Oxford to get some respite from the Blitz. They were able to stay with Mann's father and aunt, and Francis could work in the Codrington Law Library. In the London nights when sleep was hard to come by, he took his turn with fire-watching or worked at abstruse problems of law. Friends were often staying in their house, among them Otto Kahn-Freund, with whom he sometimes played chess during the night. Like everyone else who lived through the air raids, the Manns were impressed by the stoicism and nonchalance of those brought together by the common experience of danger. There was, Mann felt, a real spiritual strength in the country.

Their third child, Nicola, was born in June 1944 after her brother and sister had returned, and when the guided missiles known as V1's or "doodlebugs" were falling on London. Mann went with his wife by ambulance to the nursing home and left her with her obstetrician to begin a long walk home in the small hours. There was no one about, just sporadic explosions. He walked for an hour or so before a stray taxi picked him up. "Have you been a bad boy?" the driver asked. When he explained that nothing could have been further from the truth, the cabby willingly took him far off his own route home through the noisiest part of that night's raid.

V

Money

While Mann was pondering his career prospects in England against the possibility that he and Lore might never be granted naturalisation, he decided to enter for the LLM course at the London School of Economics. It might gain time with the Home Office, and it would keep alive the chance of the academic future which had always been his chosen objective. His fellow students on the course included Otto Kahn-Freund, and Joseph Gold, later legal adviser to the International Monetary Fund, and he had the absorbing and formative experience of being taught English Legal History by Theodore Plunkett. But when he took the examination in 1935 he failed. A second attempt the following year succeeded.

By that time he had decided to write a book on the law of money. He never explained the origins of that pregnant decision. One reason must have been his academic ambition. As one of his German academic colleagues said, with perhaps more insight than accuracy, to receive a doctorate even an English lawyer must write a book – and that might be the reason why there are so few legal doctors in England. Mann wanted to achieve academic recognition here, and he intended to submit the book as a doctoral thesis. But why money? There are a few clues. His grandfather Benjamin Mann, whom he remembered as a kindly and dignified old gentleman and who had died when he was only 10, had been a partner in the banking firm of Mann and Loeb of Frankenthal. When he was 20, Mann had worked for a spell in the bank and a certificate dated April 1928 records that he had acquitted himself with distinction.   Karl Helfferich, his father's friend who had contributed to the solution of the great German inflation of 1923, and Martin Wolff had each written treatises on the law of money. Both are referred to in each of the successive editions of Mann's own book.

However that may be, on 15 December 1937 he wrote to the Clarendon Press out of the blue, without any introduction to smooth the path, to ask whether they would be prepared to publish a book which he had just completed. Its title was "The Legal Aspect of Money – with special reference to Comparative and Private International Law" and he described it as aiming to give a comprehensive and systematic treatment to the subject, "built up on a broad comparative basis". He told the Press that it was about 400 pages of foolscap and intended to be submitted as a thesis for a Doctorate in Law to London University. He added that the subject matter was then of great practical importance and that there was no rival work in the sphere of Anglo-American law. He would be glad to call on the Press and bring the manuscript along.

The reaction of the Press was interesting. Mann was not altogether unknown to them. They had declined a proposal from him as early as January 1934 (less than 6 months after he had arrived in England as a refugee) to produce a translation of the new German Company Law with a commentary, and he had himself told them that an article of his own on private international law had been published in the latest volume of the prestigious British Year Book of International Law. But he had no sort of established reputation, he was writing in a language that was not his own, and the subject of his proposal was *terra incognita*.

The reply from the Press asked Mann to forward the manuscript, but please not to trouble to call at the moment. The book was then sent successively to Mr A E Feaveryear, a Treasury official and the author of *The Pound Sterling* (a book commended in Mann's preface as "short but excellent"); Professor D J Llewellyn Davies of Birmingham University, whose seminars Mann had attended at the London School of Economics and who was selected in the absence of Dr G C Cheshire, the celebrated Oxford academic lawyer; and Sir Paul Harvey, the creator of *The Oxford Companion to English Literature*. A distinguished trio indeed. Feaveryear was to consider the financial and economic aspects of the book, Llewellyn Davies the private international law, and Harvey the prose. The process necessarily took a little while, and when Mann enquired about progress, he was informed that the Press had not been negligent.

Feaveryear thought that Mann had written a pioneer work, but he told the Press that he did not know how it was to be adequately criticised, for "I do not think there are yet any practising specialists in this branch of the law". He nevertheless thought the book merited most careful consideration. There was nothing in it to which an economist could take exception. From a naturally cautious Treasury official this amounted to a green light, and so the Press read it. Llewellyn Davies was prepared to be more positive. He thought that Mann had done his work with extraordinary thoroughness and that there was no question about his accuracy. It was a work of high quality, but the style was a bit stiff and there were "some constructions which have an alien character".

On this last the Press awaited Sir Paul Harvey's august opinion. But they were ready to make an offer of publication before they received it. This they did at the end of March 1938, at the same time telling Mann that they thought the work might benefit from some stylistic polish.   Their offer was accepted by return of post.   Harvey however did not quite agree with the criticism of the English style.   His judgement was both practical and sympathetic.   In the nature of things, he wrote to the Press, a technical legal treatise could not run as smoothly as, for instance, a work of history.   Provisos and restrictions were unavoidable, so was some jargon which would be repugnant to the ordinary reader.   The most that could be asked was that the meaning should be able to be grasped by those for whom it was intended. Mann's book, he considered, met this test, and he made only few detailed suggestions.

Mann always took great care with the style in which he wrote.   He considered that the English used by the judges was normally exemplary, and that of Lord Denning beyond compare.   He rightly feared a steady deterioration of style in the legal profession and thought this due more than anything else to the habit of dictating rather than writing by hand.   Valentine Holmes was one of his heroes and Mann recalled that he wrote out every pleading (that stilted but supreme exercise in precision and conciseness) in his own handwriting.   All Mann's writings which were to be published were first sketched in manuscript and then typed.

So the book was accepted by "the remarkable Mr. Kenneth Sisam" of the Clarendon Press, as Mann described him, and went forward to the public with very little alteration in the autumn of 1938.   The preface bore the date 12 October, as did all subsequent editions, the anniversary of the author's wedding.

It was the foundation of Mann's later reputation.   By the time the fifth, posthumous, edition came from the Press, the blurb declared that he was "considered to be one of the finest British lawyers of this century"; and the book had become the leading work on the law of money in the world and had been translated into German and Spanish. Since it was about English law, its world reputation gave a boost to England and its legal tradition.

By any reckoning the original as it was submitted to the Clarendon Press was an astonishing achievement. Here was an author brought up to write in another language and in a wholly different legal culture who, within five years of arrival in this country, was producing a ground-breaking text book in the idiom and tradition of the common law. If there were any doubt about the work's quality and aptness for the author's new environment, it was quickly dispelled by the reviewers. These were as distinguished as the Press' readers: Professor H C Gutteridge, Professor of Comparative Law at Cambridge, Professor R S T Chorley, whose Chair was in Commercial and Industrial Law at the London School of Economics, and Otto Kahn-Freund.[23] Their verdict was unanimous. Gutteridge called the treatise "a monument of erudition", while Chorley said prophetically of the book: "should it have the good fortune to come into the hands of the legal profession both among the bar and in the judiciary, [it] may well help to mould our law in the desired direction."

The book was favoured by fortune. It defied the old convention that living authors should not be cited in Court. "The Legal Aspect of Money" was cited even in the House of Lords while Mann was very much alive. His German students laughed at the old rule, but he thought there might be some sense in it after all. He knew of

---

[23] *7 Cambridge Law Journal* (1941) 166; 3 *Modern Law Review* (1940) 331; 57 *Law Quarterly Review* (1941) 149.

instances of lawyers in Germany publishing articles – for money – in order to influence the outcome of pending cases. When you know that, Mann said, you will at least concede this much: recent writings may, depending on the identity of the author, have to be treated with a measure of circumspection.

The law of money was an unworked field. Decades of currency stability in England and the other trading nations through the nineteenth century and down to the first world war had meant that few problems had arisen for the courts to resolve. Sterling in particular was considered immutable, the currency "of whose true fixed and constant quality there is no fellow in the firmament". So, while questions could and did arise about the recovery in England of debts denominated in other currencies, it was not thought conceivable that the internal value of the pound could vary much. Sir Thomas Scrutton put it characteristically: "A pound in England is a pound whatever its international value."[24]

In any case, money in its intangible sense was considered by lawyers to be mysterious and highly theoretical, a subject fit for economists and no one else. Lawyers were distrustful of something which seemed to have little or no practical application and they were oblivious of the difficulties which it was capable of causing in their own science. Only those who had lived through a period of turbulence or raging inflation could appreciate how money stood as representative for the economic force which, as Professor Chorley remarked in his review, mankind had not yet been able to control and which could bring a people to the verge of moral and material ruin. It was one of Mann's qualifications for the

---

[24] *The Baarn* [1933] P. 251, 265.

task he had undertaken that he had seen for himself the great German inflation and its consequences. He had every reason for agreeing with Chorley. "[T]he law has to accept the remarkable fact", he wrote in his preface to the third edition, "that, while man has conquered the moon, he has signally failed to conquer the problem of the value of money, its stability and its relationship with full employment, credit and economic growth."

But he was not tempted at all to speculate about economic theory. He had said at the outset that the subject matter of the book would be discussed "from a purely legal point of view". This notwithstanding that in the first chapter he set himself to deal with the very conception and intrinsic nature of money. By the time the third edition came out in 1970 he was more explicit. The book was about the law of money, he said in the preface. It was not about economics, finance, sociology, political or any other sort of history. For lawyers economic life and its incidents were only facts to be proved in court like any other. The law stood neutral. It should not participate in a debate about economic policy and should concern itself only with clarity and coherence.

But European monetary union was the one subject which provoked him to come down into the arena. In the fifth edition of his book he listed the characteristics of true monetary union: a central bank which issues the single currency that alone is legal tender throughout the union; determines the interest rate and puts into effect the expansion or reduction of credit; takes control of the member states' external debts, – "that is to say, foreign reserves and liabilities are pooled – the latter consequence being often ignored." He concluded: "There cannot, however, be any doubt that a monetary union presupposes a constitutional organisation which is or approximates that of a single (federal) state."[25]

Mann was fiercely opposed to a federal European state. He considered it was unlikely to achieve its often unstated but real object, the elimination of war from Europe and preventing the re-emergence of a dominant Germany; and he applauded Mrs Thatcher's resolute resistance to it. He exposed the pretence that the issue was one of economics only: would joining a single currency be good or bad for Britain's business health and prosperity? He considered the matter was political, first and last. In a series of letters to *The Times* he chose more forceful language than he thought seemly in a text book. "Forget the high-sounding phrases, study the facts and the aberration will become so obvious as to disappear. In short, in the sophisticated western economies, a single currency without a single state or a structure approximating to it is unlikely to be practicable." (4 June 1991).

For all his concern with clarity, Mann did not mistake the mystery of his subject. In the fifth edition he placed a medieval rhyme attributed to the Abbot of St. Martin-de-Tournai at the head of the chapter on Nominalism (the doctrine that a pound is a pound whatever may be its international value)

> En monnoies est li cose moult obscure.
> Elles vont haut et bas, se ne set-on que faire;
> Quant on guide wagnier, on trouve le contraire.

> Money and currency are most obscure things.
> They keep on going up and down and no-one knows why,
> If you want to win you lose however hard you try.

In 1938, when the book was first published, there were few English legal textbooks of quality. Most of those in

---

[25] Pages 508–9.

use today, even those which are now treated as having a respectable antiquity, remained to be written. It is against this background that "The Legal Aspect of Money" deserves to be judged. It was not like a book on, say, the law of contract in which the shape was more or less predetermined. Mann had to work out his own plan. Starting with a blank sheet, he decided to divide the subject into two main parts: English money in English domestic law, and all questions of foreign currency from an English point of view.

He found that for the fundamentals of his subject, a single seventeenth century case, *The Case of Mixed Money*[26], provided virtually the only source of information in the law reports. The facts of the case were straightforward. Gilbert of London had sold goods to Brett of Drogheda for £100 sterling "current and lawful money of England" payable at the tomb of Earl Strongbow in Dublin. Before the time for payment arrived Elizabeth had minted a quantity of "mixed" (debased) coin and by proclamation ordered it to be circulated in Ireland. The Queen's purpose was to pay the army which she had had to raise to put down the Tyrone rebellion. When the time came for payment Brett tendered the debased coin. Gilbert refused to accept it. The Chief Judges of Ireland decided that Brett had made good tender. The principle which was established, and has never since been departed from, is that the obligation to pay £100 sterling is to pay whatever the law denominates as £100 at the time of payment.

Mann discovered that when Sir John Davis wrote his report of the case more than 300 years before, he had drawn on the writings of continental scholars and if, as seemed to be so, these had been accepted into the

---

[26] *Gilbert v Brett* (1604) Davis 18; 2 State Trials 114.

common law, it followed that the sources of the English law of money were largely foreign. "This", he wrote, "may perhaps also be regarded as a justification for the fact that it is a lawyer originally trained under a foreign legal system who now ventures to revive the study of the law of money."

It was more than a justification for writing. It strongly supported the comparative basis on which Mann had laid out his work. His intimate knowledge of and copious reference to cases from the Continent and the United States were peculiarly apt in the field of money. The problems are everywhere similar. There is hardly any aspect of commercial law in which it is more valuable to have rules which are recognisable wherever merchants trade and rely on money as the means of payment. "[m]oney is a universal institution." Mann wrote. "Hence the comparative method has peculiar value. It discloses where English law has adopted the right or the wrong road."[27]

He waged one campaign to put English law on the right road over some forty years. The opening shots were fired in the first edition of "The Legal Aspect of Money". It had been traditionally impossible to recover foreign currency through the English courts. The reasons were tortuous and outdated. If someone were sued in England on a US dollar debt, the plaintiff could recover only sterling, and the debt had to be converted from dollars to sterling at the rate of exchange ruling when the debt became due. That was well and good if sterling maintained its dollar value, but what if it were devalued between the date when the debt fell due and the date when the court gave judgment? The post-war devaluations had made this more

---

[27] *The Legal Aspect of Money*, Preface to the Third Edition.

than a theoretical possibility. Through three editions of his book, Mann argued for the obvious sense of giving judgment in the currency of the debt, whatever it might be. He argued the same tirelessly in the Lord Chancellor's Private International Law Committee, the Monetary Law Committee of the International Law Association and through the Council of Europe in Strasbourg. He never gave up. Finally, in 1975, the battle for common sense and justice, as he called it, came to an end with the vindication of his point of view in the House of Lords.[28] He was to devote much of his energy, and many of his week-ends, in the years to come to writing polemics about where English law and English judges had taken the wrong, and occasionally the right, road.

Francis Mann died while he was working on the fifth edition of his book on money. He was found in bed with the proof sheets scattered around him. "For he who lives always for his studies and work does not notice when old age creeps up", Cicero had written; and Mann had quoted it in the preface to the second volume of *Studies in International Law* published only two years before.

---

[28] *Miliangos v George Frank (Textiles) Limited* [1976] AC 443.

VI

Berlin Again

In the summer of 1946 Berlin lay in ruins. The bombing campaign to destroy the morale of the people had failed but the city barely existed any more. The chaos was indescribable, incomparably worse than it had ever been in wartime London. Whole areas of the city were unrecognisable. The fabric of life had equally been destroyed. A skilled labourer would have to work 40 hours to earn the price of a pound of peas or 80 to buy a pound of flour. The market was either black or in barter or in cigarettes brought in by the occupying forces.

Mann saw it and was shocked beyond words. "It is quite impossible to find words capable of describing the utter chaos", he wrote to his wife. "People who come straight to Berlin, who are not really prepared for a scene like this, must steel themselves and collect their courage to take this plunge – as I have done it. I did not suffer a breakdown, because altogether I am like a person who is under the influence of some drug. When you stand at the Brandenburger Tor and look at the Tiergarten which has simply ceased to exist and is a flat piece of land, and then at the ruins of the Linden, you know the fate of Berlin. It will take 30–50 years ...."

In a scene which might have come from a film of the period, he watched what happened when he threw away the butt of a cigarette at a bus stop. An old man with a stick had been following him. So had a young boy. There was a loud cry. The boy got to the butt first and the old man hit him sharply across the legs with his stick. "The bus was moving, so I could do nothing."

It was a strange circumstance that took him to Berlin so soon after the war. Douglas Phillips had hardly been demobilised and rejoined Mann to resume their practice together when Sir Alfred Brown, the head of the Legal Division of the Control Commission for Germany, who knew Mann for his writings and work in international law, invited him to go to Berlin for a few months to help with the project for reforming German law and ridding it of the imprint of Nazism. In Mann's opinion the quest was futile. The prospect of English, French, American and Russian lawyers agreeing on what should be done and how to do it was remote. The Russians in particular were pathologically suspicious of any western initiative. In any case, purging the law was not simply a matter of cutting out the racist measures. The influence was all-pervasive. As early as 1932 Alfred Rosenberg, the theorist of the Nazi movement, had written in the *Völkischer Beobachter* (the Party's newspaper): "For National Socialism there is no law as such. Rather its goal is the strong German person, its belief is the protection of this German. And all law and social life, politics and economics have to fall into line with this aim."[29] What had such claptrap meant in the Third Reich? Nevertheless Mann accepted the offer at once. Having been denied the opportunity to wear uniform in wartime, he now went back to Berlin with the rank and accoutrements of a Lieutenant-Colonel.

* * *

[29] Ian Kershaw: *Hitler 1889–1936: Hubris.* page 383.

In 1946 the government of Germany was in the hands of the commanders-in-chief of the four powers, the United States, the USSR, France and the United Kingdom, who were also military governors in each of the four zones, and who acted jointly by unanimous decision through a control council in matters concerning the whole of Germany. The British zone was administered through a body called the Control Commission (British Element). The Legal Division, to which Mann was attached, was one of its branches, whose function it was to supervise the administration of justice in the zone and, jointly with the corresponding staff of the other three powers, to advise on the reforms which ought to be made to German law "to carry out allied policy" and to prepare the necessary reform laws.

Unknown to Mann, the question of the exact legal status of Germany was being discussed shortly before he arrived in Berlin. One of the Under-Secretaries at the Control Office, Mr Richard Wilberforce, took the view that at that stage imprecision was the better part of valour. Had he known, it is most unlikely that Mann would have agreed. He rarely saw any merit in imprecision. And when he returned from Berlin, he wasted no time in preparing a paper on that very subject which was read to the Grotius Society in March 1947 under the title "The Present Legal Status of Germany".[30] By that time the future Lord Wilberforce had returned to the Bar where he was to become a good friend and frequent colleague of Mann.

Irony awaited. Twenty years later, in 1964, Mann began to act for *Carl-Zeiss-Stifftung* of Heidenheim in

---

[30] *International Law Quarterly* (1947) 314; *Studies in International Law:* p. 634.

West Germany. This body had been sued for passing off by a concern with the same name in Jena which was an emanation of the German Democratic Republic in the east. The business in optical instruments was an old and famous one and both concerns claimed to be the true and only Zeiss. Mann obtained an order that the Foreign Office be asked to say whether the government of the United Kingdom recognised the German Democratic Republic.[31] The Foreign Office replied in effect, no. Armed with that answer, Mann and his counsel, Mark Littman, persuaded the Court of Appeal that the proceedings begun by *Zeiss* of Jena had been begun without valid authority and should be struck out[32]. Some barrister friends of Mann said that he had succeeded in abolishing East Germany. But the success was short-lived. The House of Lords reversed the decision and reinstated East Germany[33]. The Law Lords decided that the government of the German Democratic Republic was a subordinate body which the USSR had set up to act on its behalf. Lord Wilberforce was a party to the decision, and he described the argument based on the German Democratic Republic being unrecognised by the United Kingdom as "unduly formalistic".[34]   In 1946 Wilberforce had been against too much precision: now he was against excessive formalism. Mann was much aggrieved by what the Law Lords had done, Lord Wilberforce among them. He felt that they had allowed political reasons to interfere with the proper application of legal principles. (See also p.61 for a further discussion of the case.)

---

[31] *Carl-Zeiss Stiftung v Rayner and Keeler* [1964] 3 All ER 326.
[32] *Ibid (No. 2)* [1965] 1 All ER 300.
[33] *Ibid* [1967] 1 AC 853.
[34] *Ibid* 959.

It so happened that politics impacted on law in a dramatic way in the same year of 1946 when Mann was in Berlin. And again it arose out of the exact legal status of Germany. In the immediate aftermath of war the true nature of Hitler's Germany was at last being understood. Emotions were running high about the part played by the Swiss in sheltering the gold and other valuables looted by the Nazis and deposited in Switzerland. Swiss funds were blocked in the US and there was a black list which was causing damage to Swiss trade. The feeling among the Allies was that the Swiss were going to have to pay. Negotiations were set on foot and the tone was rough. They were described with studied understatement in the Message which the Swiss Federal Council sent to the Federal Assembly, recommending approval of the agreement which was eventually concluded on 25 May 1946, as *"parfois mouvementées et pas toujours agréables"*. The allied negotiators did not scruple to point out that if the war had ended otherwise it was hardly likely that an independent Switzerland would have survived. The Swiss bowed to the force of these circumstances. After much haggling they agreed to pay 250 million Swiss Francs to the Allies in settlement of all claims to gold acquired by Switzerland from Germany during the war. It was also agreed that all German-owned property in Switzerland should be "liquidated" and the proceeds divided between Switzerland and the Allies, who would use the money for the rehabilitation of countries devastated by the war.

Mann wrote a note on the agreement for The British Year Book of International Law under the title *German Property in Switzerland*[35]. (It would be interesting to

[35] 23 *British Year Book of International Law* (1946) 354.

know whether it was written while he was in Berlin.) He acknowledged that the Allies' right to claim restitution of the gold looted by the Nazis during the war and exported to Switzerland was indisputable. He concentrated instead on the seizure and sale of German-owned property in Switzerland. He pointed out that as the war was over, the Allies did not claim title to the German property either as belligerents or as victors. They claimed by reason of the capitulation of Germany in 1945 and the exercise by them of sovereign power in Germany.[36] They claimed to stand in the shoes of Germany. They could not, therefore, do more than Germany itself could have done in peacetime; and there could be no doubt, he said, that German legislation confiscating German property in Switzerland would not have been recognised by the Swiss courts. In purporting to deal with German property in Switzerland in this way, the Allies had embarked upon what he called a "probably unique extension" of international confiscation. He ended the note: "The international lawyer should remember that hard cases make bad law. The value of the Agreement as a precedent may still have to stand the test of time."

Retribution was in the forefront of everyone's mind, recompense (so far as it could humanly be made) for the war crimes of the Nazis and their accomplices. The emotions that had been aroused blotted out other thoughts,

---

[36] Mann's view was that the four allied powers had not assumed territorial sovereignty over Germany, but they that they had "jointly assumed governmental sovereignty 'with respect to Germany'". "They have reserved to themselves supreme authority over Germany's external affairs, but have delegated the exercise of 'supreme authority in Germany' to the four Commanders-in-Chief'". See *The Present Legal Status of Germany: International Law Quarterly* (1947) 314; *Studies in International Law* page 634.

but Mann's voice urged that the law should not fall silent. It was a lonely voice and a striking example, from early in his career, of something which ran like a thread through his writings: the law should never yield to political or other extraneous considerations. In another article he contributed the next year, 1947, he returned to the Swiss Agreement. "In the last resort, a choice between values has to be made: is it preferable to give overriding effect to the political considerations and to take German property in neutral countries, or to sacrifice this political aim for the sake of the principle that confiscation has no extra-territorially recognizable impact?" It is a question, he said regretfully, to which a lawyer can contribute but little.[37]

* * *

It was a brilliantly sunny day in July when Mann landed by air in Berlin. He sat down at once to write his impressions for his wife. He had already been to see the houses where they had each lived. His had had a direct hit and was destroyed, hers was damaged. The sights and sounds of the ruined city overwhelmed him. His heart was too full, his mind bewildered, for him to do more than record factually what he saw. Later he hoped to analyse his thoughts and "assess values"; but he never did.

On the first day he saw a notice of a concert that evening in what had been the comfortable residential suburb of Dahlem. He decided to go. It was in the library of a large house. There were neither roof nor windows but the room was packed. Players from the Berlin Philharmonic Orchestra performed the Schubert Octet

---

[37] *German External Assets*: 24 *British Year Book of International Law* (1947) page 239, 255.

and the Beethoven Septet. The intense concentration of players and listeners and the glory of the music brought tranquillity to the room. Outside there was despair and destruction. It was the last and most overpowering of his impressions of that first day before he went home to try to get some sleep.

The letters from Berlin are a unique series. Later in life, he wrote fewer personal letters and when he did, he used a pithy style suitable for post cards or the smaller size of notepaper. But now he wrote at length, discursively, and sometimes more than once a day. He said he felt the need late at night "to talk to you a bit", to open his feelings to her. He visited the Wannsee one afternoon and thought of the happy times they had spent together on those waters, and he told her that he wished that she and the children could have been there with him then. "The glory of the waters round Berlin makes one forget all the misery of this desolate town." But Lore did not appear to respond as sympathetically as he must have hoped. Perhaps it is not surprising. He lived in Berlin in a comfortable flat with a "bedwoman" to look after him, was going to parties and concerts and eating excellent food and drinking good wine. She was left behind in a Britain suffering the privations of post-war austerity with a young family to look after, and was being asked to keep an eye on the Norfolk Street practice as well.

The Berlin office was not to Mann's liking. There was an overweening pretence of rank, and it was riddled with intrigue. It was his first experience of office politics and he despised it. If he was outranked at a meeting, he was expected to remain silent and allow his superior officer to do all the talking. Macaskie, the chief, whose main qualification for the job was an imposing presence, was a pompous fool who was never there; his deputy, Pereira, was infatuated with his personal assistant, "a saucy girl with whom for unknown reasons I have not found favour." This outfit is rotten, he told Lore, with the exception of a Mauritius ex-judge who was badly overworked and "queer beyond description by anybody other than a Balzac or a Dickens." He did not suffer in silence and this made him something of an outsider. His experience and ability were under-used and he complained of having nothing to do. There was also a rigid rule against "fraternisation" with Germans which made it impossible to recruit help for the Legal Division from German academics, however clean their record might be. "The English are completely aloof and free from any contact with Germans", he wrote. "It is India all over again and I have to be very careful not to get into the position in which the hero of 'Passage to India' found himself."

These were unhappy circumstances. But towards the end of his spell in Berlin he was invited to dinner at the Savoy Hotel. It was an excellent dinner and very nice altogether, he told his wife. Richard Wilberforce, the Under-Secretary who, unknown to Mann, had advised against too precise a definition of the legal status of Germany, was there. He found that Wilberforce thoroughly agreed with him about the quality of the Berlin office – "a man with a very high position ... quite outspoken ... I had the satisfaction, at last, to be treated in an adequate manner." To be treated in an adequate manner was always of great importance. It was understandable in someone who had had to build a new life on the ruins of the old. It was a trait of character too. Mann knew the quality of his work and he needed to feel that it was appreciated.

There were other frustrations. The committees to reform German law were attended by representatives of each of the four occupying powers, and it was impossible to do business with the Russians, who politicised every issue, however trivial. "It is simply preposterous to think that we could ever co-operate with them. Their obstinacy, narrow-mindedness and rigidity, not to say stupidity, are too much for me and all of us." He had suddenly come very close to the deep gulf between East and West. There was barbarism on the other side and no treaty or understanding could close the gap. Then, towards the end of his tour of duty he went to a concert of Russian songs given by a Russian state choir. As usual, music touched him at the deepest level. It was music in its purest form, he wrote; he had never heard such singing by male voices.

The very experience of being in Berlin carried a poignant charge. As well as investigating the state of German law, Mann carried out his own research into the human effects of the Third Reich on its subjects. He looked up as many of his former friends and colleagues as he could and saw for himself how they had fared. From these encounters, some of them heart-rending, he saw how harsh and misguided it was to condemn the silently compliant, the apathetic and those who had looked the other way; and how rare were the anti-Nazis, as distinct from the non-Nazis.

He went to see Suse Meyer, Lore's cousin. Her husband, a journalist, had suffered a stroke as a result of *Kristallnacht* in 1938 when many Jews were sent to the camps. He was unfit to travel and she nursed him until he died in 1942, so escaping transportation. She then had to go underground, zigzagging across Germany from one hiding place to another and evading one betrayal after another. She was helped in this desperate enterprise by her landlord in Berlin who was a hairdresser and an "Aryan". She posed as his fiancée with false papers that he had procured for her. "Personally I had little to lose, apart from my life," she wrote afterwards. Her husband was dead, her only son was in England, the rest of her family had been taken away to an unknown fate. Her only concern was to avoid doing anything to endanger those who were helping her. Right up to the end, even in the chaos of 1945, she had to keep out of the way of informers, "the self-important busybodies" as she called them, who were still at work. In the last phase while she was in the east of the country she had an experience that shocked even her. Everyone had gone, the Russians were close, and two young German soldiers were there as rearguard look-outs. She and others were sitting in the parlour of an inn with them, trying to get them to save their lives by getting rid of their weapons. To no avail. One of them, an intelligent young man of 25 or so with wife and child, continued to spout the Nazi ideology of Alfred Rosenberg. Even in that final moment, as she described it, he "took the whole nonsense seriously enough to be willing to give up his life for it".

She survived, returned to Berlin, and married the hairdresser to whose courage and selflessness she owed her life. When Mann saw her, he found her unchanged, even looking younger and happy. "But", he confided to Lore, "the problems are there all right." She had married "this quite proletarian and uneducated man *um sich zu revanchieren* [to repay a debt], an expression she let fall in a not quite remote connection."

He sought out Eduard Kohlrausch, whose Faculty Assistant Lore had been, and who had been Rector of Berlin University. The Kohlrausch family lived in the Russian sector of Berlin. Conditions were dreadful and a bitter little rhyme was circulating.

Lieber Gott, gib uns das Fünfte Reich
Das Vierte ist dem Dritten gleich

Dear God – give us the Fifth Reich,
The Fourth is the same as the Third.

He found Kolrausch aged, short-sighted and hard of hearing. He had been detained by the Russians on doubts about his past but was then released and reinstated. Mann was much impressed by his wife, thin and white, "but still a great lady of the best German bourgeois type". She was going out into the country daily with a rucksack on her back to collect potatoes. They accepted Mann's small gifts with dignity. He was impressed too by Kohlrausch's mental vitality and erudition.   They talked about German history, the great legal writers, even Bracton. The atmosphere was unchanged and *herzlich*. Their condemnation of Nazism was loud and, Mann thought, "largely genuine, particularly in so far as Jews are concerned ... but the hopelessness of their situation is overpowering, and my feeling also is that they make a sharp distinction between Nazis and the German people (including the *Wehrmacht*) which I cannot accept and which we did not discuss. They did say, however, that there were so few Nazis! It is a wall of protection and justification which they build for themselves."

He saw Eduard Wahl against whom he had debated at his doctoral ceremony. Wahl was in a poor state. His wife had died and his young children were undernourished and tubercular. Although he had been a Party member (involuntarily, so he said) he had been "de-Nazified" because of an obscure connection with the failed plot to kill Hitler in 1944, and reinstated as a Professor at Heidelberg. He was later to become a member of the Federal Parliament. "He is a real German" Mann commented, "with that typical *Wehleidigkeit* (self-pity) and incapacity of seeing or believing in the suffering of others." He was violently anti-Russian and proud of the achievements of the Germans. He dumbfounded Mann by saying during their conversation about the war, "Yet, you know, great things were done." To his wife Mann wrote: "I am certain he would give a second Hitler another chance." But he went on to say that the utter hopelessness of the man made a deep impression on him and "since I am weak, evoked my sympathy."

He added, presciently, that in spite of the hopelessness all round him in Berlin, "Yet I for one am sure that they will recover – their efficiency, industry, cleanliness is something that always amazes me."

Here in the shattered city with its broken lives Mann saw with his own eyes the final working out of Hitler's revolution. He could have been forgiven if he had dismissed with contempt the insensitivity and special pleading that he encountered. He did not. The wretched condition to which these Berliners had been reduced moved him to sympathy; and after that experience he could not condemn those whose worst crime was to have averted their eyes and preferred to get on with the business of living their daily lives.

He visited his father's old housekeeper who was living in Frankfurt. Richard, who had been in England since 1938, was continuing to pay her a pension. She had been Mann's nanny and was delighted to see him again. "I could write volumes about Lydia who is the only real anti-Nazi (as opposed to a non-Nazi) I have met here." She was fiercely uncompromising about the Nazis and their sympathisers: *"Ihr habt's ja nicht anders gewollt, und jetzt wollt ihr auch noch gut fressen"* (You didn't want it any other way – and yet you now want to gorge yourself with food), she said contemptuously. Since she had kept company with Jews and those of mixed blood (*mischlings*) she was suspected of having Jewish blood herself. Her reply was simply that she was a person of integrity. She did not complain about anything, was managing quite well and was happy that the war was lost. Why are the women so much stronger than the men? Mann asked his wife.

The black and white cases were easy. On the one side, the Lydias, who were rare; on the other hand, those who carried on their sleeve the badge of guilt. He described how one day he had run into one such, a man called Reuss, who had been an Assistant in the law faculty with him. "We recognised each other: He: "*Wir kennen uns doch.*" I: "*Wir haben uns einmal gekannt.*" ("Don't we know each other?" "We knew each other once.") It was dismissive. They talked for a while. Reuss asked after Lore Ehrlich and others he had known. He emphasised his own Anti-Nazism. Mann knew better and remembered the articles which Reuss had written for the *Juristiche Wochenschrift* (the same journal for which Mann had written his first article) when it had later acquired a notorious Nazi slant. It makes you sick, he wrote. Some of his friends could not understand how Mann could submit himself to this sort of thing, so soon after the nightmare had ended. They thought his curiosity morbid.

But where was the line of guilt to be drawn? In his letters home he wrestled with the question. He knew that the genuine anti-Nazis were few and far between. A vast majority were either active supporters or complicit or pliant. Membership of the Party would not do as a test. It was mechanical and superficial. Some had joined to protect their families; others had joined in the last years of the régime when things had become "far too complicated for such crude distinctions". And what to do about the

German nationalists, "patriots", militarists and soldiers? The problem was an impossible one. Germany could not be kept in bondage. The only solution was "control at the top but let them lead their lives. Forget the past except in so far as the real criminals are concerned. These should be hanged."

But who were they? He thought there were many hundreds of thousands of real Nazis, most still in their places: those who brought the regime to power, but not all those who were or became *Mitläufer* (time-servers). There were too many of them and that was the practical difficulty. He was beginning to go round in circles in his grapple with the problem of the guilt of a nation. It was Burke, one of his heroes, who had said, "I do not know the method of drawing up an indictment against an whole people." He told his wife he could not discuss it anymore and had to go to bed. So he would end his letter.

While Mann was in Berlin the trial of the Nazi leaders was reaching its final stage in Nuremberg. No anxieties about whether the right defendants were in the dock arose here. He found that he had an opportunity to go and told Lore that he could not describe how much he was looking forward to it. By chance Goering was giving evidence on one of the days he was in court. Mann was compelled in spite of himself and he had to concede that Goering "dominates the box and the Defence ... there is no doubt that he is a personality of great force and demonic evil, while all the others are non-entities to a really amazing degree."

He was at first impressed by the judicial atmosphere. He had had doubts if it was wise to stage a trial in this form, but they disappeared when he felt the atmosphere, because it was a real trial. Sir Geoffrey Lawrence, the

British presiding judge, was not outstanding, but he was a Judge, and that was the important thing from the point of view of history and public opinion. But in his next letter he had, he said, to revise his view. Lawrence was a disappointment, he was erratic and not always fair. The Americans were "a poor lot, and altogether one cannot say that the trial has been provided with that amount of brilliant talent which the occasion would have deserved." Moreover, the attempt to establish criminality against whole organisations, such as the SS, was "an impossible proposition". It was a political decision and the material was too vast for any court to handle.

When the judgments became known Mann was surprised that Papen (Chancellor just before Hitler, Vice-Chancellor afterwards 1933–4, and diplomat) and Schacht (President of the Reichsbank and financier of the regime) had been acquitted, and he told Lore that he had not expected that so many would be sent to prison only. He doubted whether the judges had really mastered the mass of material and thought perhaps that the verdicts had been arrived at "by some crude method". The German press also was critical of the acquittals. "But", he wrote, "the whole problem of this trial is squarely put by these cases: Schacht and Papen were politically guilty. Were they legally guilty?" These were the difficulties which every lawyer knew. But what else could be done but try the Nazi leaders? Mann never doubted that it was right to do so.

Altogether, it was an overwhelming – and exhausting – experience for him to see the gangsters in the box. He thought a lot about her, he told Lore in a letter written in the evening after he had been in court. "I am not enough of a writer (and am too tired) to give an adequate expression to all my impressions and feelings, – there are by far too many, and the concentration of exciting experiences is almost too much. I do think that if I could talk to you and live through these days with you, it would help a lot, but also make me happier."

* * *

The meetings with people he had known in another world, and perhaps also the experience of the Nuremberg trial, turned Mann's mind to other things. While he was in Frankfurt in August, 1946 on the way to Nuremberg he met "His Magnificence" (as he called him) Walter Hallstein for the first time since Mann's university days. He told his wife that Hallstein "in all probability will ask me to give a lecture in Marburg and one in Frankfurt" the following month. He did give some lectures and also held discussion groups in Marburg in September and reported that he found it a most interesting experience. "I came into contact with German students and professors this morning. I even saw something of the terrible problems of the refugees from the East. There are 7½ million of these people and the misery of these people surpasses anything I have yet seen." The lectures went well, he thought. "I was strictly legal, academic, scientific, objective." He did not, as others did, allow the lectures to degenerate into political discussions. That was not what the students wanted. "They want to learn. They want facts, not words the futility of which is too obvious for them." He began to think that academics with his background had a responsibility to assist in the rebuilding of Germany.

These views were strengthened during a visit which he made to Germany in the Spring of 1948 while he was acting for Baron Thyssen-Bornemisza and attempting to negotiate the release of the Thyssen steel interests from Allied military control. He was in Düsseldorf staying comfortably at the Park Hotel, when he met his old friend Werner Flume. It was a memorable meeting and the first for fifteen years, when Flume had been a witness at his marriage. Flume had spoken up publicly against a Nazi call for students to boycott lectures by Jewish Professors in the law faculty of Berlin University and had angrily refused to join the Party. As a result he had forfeited the academic career for which he had seemed predestined. Mann was not allowed to take his friend into his hotel, which was reserved for allied personnel, and he could not take him to a restaurant because, as a visitor, he did not have a German ration book. So he and Flume walked the streets of the city, talking, as he recalled later.

> We discussed not only the past but also the future, – his, mine, Germany's. We analysed the enormous and challenging task that lay ahead. It became very clear to me that people, particularly academics in my position and with my background had a considerable responsibility towards Germany. German youth was, and was likely to be, cut off from the developments in the West. Twelve years had to be made good. The right direction had to be shown. Young Germans had never met a Jew. Hitler's errors had to be shown up by the living example. The ideals of the rule of law, of justice and law had to be revived. The task was enormous, promising and multifarious.

The meeting with Flume may have had a further significance. Flume resumed academic life in the law faculty of Bonn University in 1954. He could not return to Berlin because the old University was in the Russian sector of the city. It was he who prepared the ground at Bonn for Mann to be appointed an Honorary Professor there in 1960. It is speculation but the two old friends may have realised that the appointment could bring incidental benefits to both the University and Mann. Flume and those at Bonn of like mind would have wanted German university life to return to normal after the aberration of the Hitler years. They would have wanted to reclaim the old intellectual traditions. The return of a Jewish refugee to teach would be a dramatic way for the University to demonstrate its intentions. On Mann's part, teaching regularly would enhance his reputation in Germany to the advantage of his German-based practice.

From 1946 Mann lectured at German universities. There was hardly any German university where he did not give a lecture. From 1960 onwards he gave a course of lectures every year at Bonn on English law and on international commercial law, and held a seminar on the latter subject until 1988. At the end of his days he looked back on this work "with a measure of satisfaction". As well he might. The work which he did, and the reasons which animated him, were rare among the refugee academics of his generation. Mann was one of the few who felt that "rebuilding a sound intellectual standard in Germany" was a duty which ought to be discharged.

The experience of Berlin in 1946 was a crucial one. Looking back over his life it emerges as the episode which linked two worlds. Had it not been for the invitation to join the Allied Control Commission he might never have started to teach in Germany.   Seeing Berlin then, with everything he had known and touched destroyed, made him a witness to the incalculable loss which Germany had sustained; and it stirred in him the thought that there might be something he could do. Without that experience he might have turned his back forever, professionally and emotionally, on the country of his birth, as so many refugees did.

VII

Writings

Francis Mann pursued his academic interests of writing and thinking about law in almost complete isolation. His intellectual loneliness, he admitted, was at all times more serious than his friends could imagine. He did not have the support or resources of a university, or academic colleagues with whom he could discuss his ideas and test them against criticism. Instead, he worked alone in libraries on Saturdays or at home in the evenings. It is the more remarkable that he produced writings of such imagination and insight. And it is the sadder that he was deprived in England of the opportunity to teach that he had in Germany.

There was a hidden blessing in the solitary life. He had complete freedom and independence to write what he liked, was never beholden to anyone, and never wanted anything from anyone. His writing is the best warrant that, as he put it, he did not have to look right or left. It is not likely that the narrowness and leisured pace which characterises much of university life could have provided him with the sort of stimulus he needed. By his own account, almost all his academic work was provoked by his experience as a practitioner, and many of his most important cases would not have reached him but for his writings. The two sides of his work became interdependent. Neither could satisfy him by itself. He explained how the relationship between the two worked out.

Purely academic law is liable to become sterile.   The demands of an extensive practice are such that they always lead to some fruitful starting point for research. It is rare that practice directly brings up the wish to explore a particular problem.   What arises in practice is usually on the fringe of some central topic. Or when reading something up for the purpose of solving a specific, probably very narrow problem, one suddenly comes across or sees a much wider subject worthy of exploration. But it is life in practice that provides the fertile ground ...

Mann was a true jurist.   The combination of a life in practice with university teaching and writing was in the Berlin tradition of Savigny in which he had been brought up.   That was how he had planned to spend the rest of his life in Germany. And that was how he was thought of in England when, at the end of his life, he was belatedly honoured. In 1989, he was given an Honorary Doctorate by Oxford University, and the University Orator hit the point. "Should he not therefore be classed as an academic, one of the throng so well represented here? Yet he belongs to another throng, those lawyers who practise daily in the law courts. He is really like Plato's *Diotima*, that spirit who reconciles gods and men by interpreting 'to the gods what men are saying and to men what the gods are saying'."

But there was little scope for any interpreting of that sort when he began to practise in England almost fifty years earlier; little commerce between lawyers in the universities on one hand, and those at the Bar or on the Bench on the other. It must have been incomprehensible to him. Everything he had learnt in Germany ran counter. He found that in England judges and practitioners often regarded the work of academics as speculations which had little or no relevance to actual cases. The outlook of the profession was that you learned by experience. A day in court was worth many a text book and innumerable lectures. It was not considered helpful for an advocate to refer the court to academic writings. "Can I look at this book?" a judge once asked counsel in 1936, observing that he understood it was court practice only to read works written by members of the Bar.[38] And, by a bizarre convention which Mann did much to break by his own efforts, living authors were not permitted to be cited at all. In spite of Mann's own explanation of the rule (see page 57), what was really the sanctity supposed to be conferred by death? In response, academics were apt to think that the judges did not fully understand the principles they were supposed to be applying. This inhospitable climate changed and improved only slowly during Mann's working life. He contributed much to the change.

Mann's old friend and sparring partner, Otto Kahn-Freund, wrote to him from what he conceived to be the disadvantaged position of London University, but also with the objectivity of someone brought up in a different tradition. There was no dignity attached to academic law in England, Kahn-Freund said. The real rulers of the profession "imbibe" law. They don't have to read it because what matters is the atmosphere. That was in 1959. Whether or not Mann agreed with this ironic but depressing analysis, it did not stop him from writing that others might read. By the seventies Mann thought that the influence of law teachers had begun to penetrate the consciousness of Bench and Bar. And certainly one article he wrote in 1973 had an immediate and dramatic effect on a current case.[39]

[38] Mr Justice Clauson in *Re Thompson* [1936] Ch. 676, 680.

[39] *Oppenheimer v Cattermole* [1972] Ch. 585; [1973] Ch. 264 (CA); [1976] AC 249. For a full account of the case see Lawrence Collins: *Dr F A Mann: His Work and Influence*. The British Year Book of International Law (1993) 102.

Mr Oppenheimer was a Jew who had been born in Germany in 1896. He was a victim of Nazi persecution and came to settle in England in 1939. He applied successfully for British nationality in 1948. The question was whether he was exempt from UK tax on a pension paid by the German government for the work he had done before he left Germany as a teacher in a Jewish orphanage. For this he had to establish that he had retained his German nationality notwithstanding that a Nazi decree of 1941 had deprived Jews of their nationality. So it seemed that the English courts would have to decide whether to give effect to these Nazi decrees, or whether they could bring themselves to declare that racist-inspired law, wherever made, should not be accorded validity in England. The Court of Appeal decided that however odious was the Nazi decree, effect would nonetheless have to be given to it.[40]

This dreadful decision provoked Bernard Levin to write a piece for *The Times* under the heading, "If the law supposes that, the law *ist ein esel*". When Mann read the decision he at once wrote an article for the *Law Quarterly Review*[41]. He was always ready to seize the opportunity given by a flawed decision. The article pointed out circumstances that had not been considered at all by the Court. One was that the constitution of the Federal Republic enabled those like Mr. Oppenheimer, who had been deprived of their citizenship on racial

[40] This was the view of two of the judges, Lords Justices Orr and Buckley. Lord Denning considered that the Nazi decree was not entitled to recognition ("an objectionable and atrocious law") but that Mr Oppenheim lost his German nationality by applying for naturalisation.

[41] *The Present Validity of Nazi Nationality Laws:* 89 Law Quarterly Review (1973) 194.

grounds, to apply for a re-grant of German nationality. Mr. Oppenheimer had not done so. Then he described how the Federal Supreme Court, "to their everlasting credit", had decided that the Nazi decrees were null and void, as lacking "the quality of law". Finally he referred to an earlier German law of 1913, still in force, by which German nationals lost their nationality on acquiring another one, as Mr. Oppenheimer had done by becoming British by naturalisation. It followed that if the Nazi decree of 1941 were recognised by the English courts, Mr. Oppenheimer lost his German nationality then. If it were not recognised, then he lost it when he became a British subject in 1948. Either way, he would lose his case and have to pay tax.

Unknown to Mann, Oppenheimer had appealed to the House of Lords and the hearing had concluded. At this point Mann met Lord Hodson, one of the Law Lords who had heard the appeal, at a reception. To Mann's amazement, he began to talk about the case and told him that he had already written his own speech in favour of allowing the appeal. Mann told him about his article. Later he was told by another Law Lord, Lord Salmon, that he had read Mann's article as soon as it appeared and, having done so, had told his colleagues that they should consider reversing the decision they had previously reached. As a direct result of these events the hearing was re-opened, and the case was sent back to the Special Commissioners, the tribunal of first instance. After a delay of more than a year, the case returned to the Lords and was decided in accordance with Mann's argument.

This was an unprecedented state of affairs. A newly written article in a legal periodical had caused the House of Lords to reopen a question which had been as good as closed. There were references to Mann's article in the

Law Lords' speeches. He had had a great success. But he was not overwhelmed with pleasure: he considered the acknowledgement "very restrained". What must have pleased him more, though, was that the final decision made clear, and two of the Law Lords, Lords Cross and Salmon, declared in terms that "laws" like the Nazi decree of 1941 were a violation of human rights and ought not to be dignified by recognition in English Courts.

There had been two judges in the Court of Appeal, Lords Justices Buckley and Orr, and one in the House of Lords, Lord Pearson, who had insisted on giving effect to the Nazi decree. "The typically positivistic attitude of the English lawyer" was how Mann disparaged this sort of view. "It is probably due to the deep-seated, though wholly mistaken, belief in the inexorable omnipotence of Parliament or, indeed, of any lawgiver, which prevents any kind of judicial review." He waged a long war against this attitude and it brought out some of his best polemical writing. Courts, he argued, must be willing to strike down oppressive or barbarous decrees, wherever they might be found, and uphold human rights.

In 1959 Mann had thought that "restraint and a constant respect for propriety are more effective protectors of fundamental rights than laws or even constitutions, which frequently are mere technical instruments in the hands of lawyers and in any case are liable to be changed."[42] But as time went on he came to believe that a Bill of Rights was needed. In 1978 he gave the Blackstone lecture under the title "Britain's Bill of Rights"[43] and made it clear that he thought it was high time to introduce one. He was early

---

[42] *Outlines of a History of Expropriation: 75 Law Quarterly Review* (1959) 188.

[43] 94 *Law Quarterly Review* (1978) 512; *Further Studies in International Law,* page 103.

in the field in calling for a code of fundamental human rights to form part of English law. The obstacle to reform, as Mann saw it, was a mixture of complacency and the rigidly held doctrine of parliamentary supremacy. According to this doctrine parliament is omnipotent. There is no higher law. Because its power knows no bounds a later parliament can undo anything done by an earlier one. So no law can be permanent. No court can enquire whether a statute passed by parliament infringes any fundamental human right. If a judge did so he would usurp the function of parliament.

It follows that if these notions are accepted, a code of fundamental rights, which might be thought congenial to the English tradition of liberty, cannot be embedded permanently into our law. Mann did not agree and called these propositions "peculiarly English doubts".[44] We cannot possibly assume, he said, that English law conforms to the standards of a Bill of Rights. And if we do have some fundamental rights in our law, they are judge-made and can be undone by parliament. It would be unrealistic to trust parliament to take care of our human rights. Suppose parliament prohibited marriages between different faiths or races, would English judges have to apply that law? "Do not evade the issue, do not avoid the legal test by asserting that, as we all hope and believe, no English Parliament would ever pass such a statute. Would the hypothetical question really have to be answered in the affirmative, while a similar German statute was condemned by four Law Lords as constituting

---

[44] He was not alone. As early as 1945, Sir Hersch Lauterpacht had proposed an international Bill of Rights to which Britain could accede in a way consistent with its constitutional history. See *An International Bill of the Rights of Man.* Columbia University Press 1945. Since publication of that work, others had taken a similar view.

"so grave an infringement of human rights that the courts of this country ought to refuse to recognise it as law at all"?[45]

He pointed out a situation of almost Gilbertian perversity. The European Convention on Human Rights had not been approved, still less ratified or adopted in a statute, by parliament. It was signed on behalf of the government, and government also – and crucially – accepted the right of individual petition to Strasbourg and the compulsory jurisdiction of the Strasbourg court. Thus the parliament which enjoys absolute supremacy has had no hand in the European Court of Human Rights becoming a court of final appeal for the United Kingdom. The upshot, said Mann, is that we trust judges sitting in Strasbourg and drawn from many diverse countries to decide whether our law or our government has infringed fundamental rights. At the same time we withhold these powers from our own judges. He ended the lecture by calling for a debate. The call was fittingly answered by Anthony Lester in the seventh F.A. Mann lecture which he gave in 1983 under the title *Fundamental Rights: The United Kingdom Isolated?*[46] It was fitting too that Lord Lester introduced a Bill which much influenced the content of the Human Rights Act, 1998. That Act finally removed the paradox to which Mann had pointed twenty years earlier. It empowers English judges for the first

---

[45] A reference to *Oppenheimer v Cattermole* (discussed above).

[46] *Public Law 1984*, 46. This article and Lord Lester's later one, U.K. *Acceptance of the Strasbourg Jurisdiction: What really went on in Whitehall in 1965: Public Law 1998*, 237, give a fascinating account of the decision – making process (if it may be so described) which led to the UK signing the European Convention and, later, accepting the jurisdiction of Strasbourg and the right of individual petition, thus creating the paradoxical situation to which Mann had drawn attention.

time to review a statute made by parliament and to decide whether or not it is compatible with fundamental human rights. It does not however empower them to strike down the offending statute.[47]   In Lord Lester's own view, the Act "subtly respects the form but not the substance of parliamentary sovereignty".[48]   We cannot know what Mann's view would have been, but without power for the judges to declare statutes invalid, he might have thought that vestiges of the "peculiarly English doubts" remained.

Mann's daily practice was not concerned with human rights and he was not a long-serving member of the campaign to bring fundamental human rights back across the English Channel and into the jurisdiction of English judges.   His contribution consisted of the Blackstone Lecture alone.   His principal concern was the threat that an unchecked executive might set human rights at nought by subverting the constitution – something that in any case he thought did not exist, or at best rested only on convention.   It should not be overlooked that when he gave his lecture a Labour government was in power in Britain.   Like Lord Hailsham, who coined his phrase, "Elective Dictatorship" a year or two earlier, his thinking was coloured by the circumstances of the time, and the apprehension that governments of the left were more threatening to the constitutional balance in Britain than the Conservatives.   Or, as he more elegantly expressed it, the product of any creation "invariably bears the stamp of the moment of creation."

[47] By the Human Rights Act, 1998, if a UK court decides that legislation is not compatible with the code of human rights incorporated in the Act, it may make a "declaration of incompatibility".   This does not affect the validity of the legislation (sections 3 and 4).   It is then for parliament to put matters right – or not.

[48] Private communication from Lord Lester.

The importance of the Blackstone Lecture is for the light it sheds on his conception of law. He considered that in its fundamentals law is paramount and immutable. In his book, *An International Bill of the Rights of Man*, written in 1945, Hersch Lauterpacht had stated that "the idea of natural and inalienable human rights is in fact a denial of the absolute supremacy of any earthly legislative power". Mann agreed, and wrote:

> Fundamental laws are not only inalienable, but, by virtue of their authority, character and content also exist independently of any text which may attempt to formulate them, and bind the community, whether or not it submits to them. The Ten Commandments are fundamental laws: their binding and lawmaking force is universal and eternal and would be so even if they had not been given formal expression.[49]

Mann considered that law should be imbued with moral purpose and never be manipulated to suit political or social ends. Not so his friend Otto Kahn-Freund, whose idea of law was diametrically different. Social policy was for him the very object of the law. As Lord Wedderburn put it in his memoir on Kahn-Freund for The British Academy, he "never tired of telling students that they must go 'through' the law to the social policy; they were not entitled to go round it."[50] Mann could not have agreed less, and they argued about it tirelessly in correspondence. It is a tribute to both men that their friendship, which went back to their days in Berlin, was never impaired.

Kahn-Freund was a gentle scholar. But he was just as immovable as Mann. He wrote of the "unbridgeable

---

[49] *The Doctrine of* Jus Cogens *in International Law: Further Studies in International Law*, page 84.

[50] Proceedings of The British Academy (1982) vol. 68, page 581.

gulf between your thinking and mine ... You really believe that a society can be governed by abstractions, whereas I believe that it is always governed by people, including those who transform crystallised abstractions into constantly varying policies." Mann replied that his friend could not avoid the crucial question by calling justice, justness, liberty, or the presumption of innocence, "abstractions". "They are fundamental requirements of law, moral, natural or legal law. And they have practical consequences for the practitioner and the academic lawyer ... We are lawyers because we believe in and uphold them. If we did not do so, we would be cynics, cynicism being the antithesis of law. This applies to you no less than to all of us, or to – Yours ever, F A M".

Kahn-Freund was a socialist pacifist who had proved his courage when he was a judge of the Labour Court in Berlin in the first months of Nazi rule. He had had to decide whether three employees of the radio service had been validly dismissed on the ground that they were Communists and had threatened to sabotage Hitler's first broadcast as Chancellor. He found no evidence to support it, whether the men were Communists or not, and reinstated them. He was speedily removed from the bench.

Mann naturally admired what his friend had done in Germany, but thought that Kahn-Freund had done harm in England by his thinking. He had, "by a sort of Damascus", discovered that British collective agreements between employees and employers were, unlike their counterparts in other countries, not legally binding because the parties did not intend them to be. Neither side intended that union agreements should be enforced in the courts. This idea, which Lord Wedderburn described as "a brilliant and intuitive rationalisation", convinced the Donovan

Royal Commission on Trade Unions and Employers Associations, and subsequently parliament. Mann thought the Donovan Report "one of the most negative, uninformed and useless documents ever produced" and the notion that labour agreements should be unenforceable a perilous heresy, just the sort of thing that happened when social policy was allowed to influence legal principle. It had the consequence of extending the already undue influence of the trade unions and perpetuating the lawless jungle of industrial relations in Britain.

On 26 January 1979, amid the misery of widespread strikes and the last agonies of the Callaghan government, Mann wrote to *The Times* (which was itself then strike-bound so that the letter had to be printed in the *Daily Telegraph*) to make his point. He contrasted the futility of the Labour government's policy of relying on codes of conduct and other non-binding devices, with the German régime of legally enforceable collective agreements. In 1973, he wrote, there had been a "go-slow" by the German air traffic controllers who were employees of the Federal Government. The government successfully sued the association to which the controllers belonged in the Federal Supreme Court, and was granted an indemnity for its liability to travel agencies and others who had suffered loss as a result of the "go-slow". "Is it not likely", Mann asked, "that the present generation of German air controllers will think hard before repeating the experiment of 1973? Is there not a lesson to be learned?"

It was only two months before the government fell and Mrs Thatcher formed her first administration after the ensuing general election. Otto Kahn-Freund died in the same summer.

For all their differences, and they were deep, Kahn-Freund admired his friend's achievements and knew that he was not flattering him when he wrote: "You have mapped out for yourself a unique position in the world of legal learning." He was one of two academics with whom Mann had a truly close friendship and with whom he carried on the academic debate that he so much craved. The other was Sir Hersch Lauterpacht. The legacy of that latter friendship is the two volumes of *Studies in International Law* which Mann published in 1973 and 1990.

Lauterpacht was ten years older than Mann and had come to England in 1923, not as a refugee, when Mann was still at school. By 1932 he had become Reader in Public International Law in London University and in 1938 was made Whewell Professor of International Law at Cambridge. No one who attended his lectures during his long tenure there until 1955 will ever forget the fervour of his advocacy for an international rule of law. Mann first met him when, after a lecture which he gave to the Grotius Society, he unexpectedly had a letter from Lauterpacht suggesting that they meet.[51] From that first approach, Mann wrote, "there stemmed a friendship which lasted, developed and grew until his premature death in 1962." The friendship was continued into the next generation by Hersch's son, Sir Elihu Lauterpacht, himself a distinguished international lawyer who in 1993 gave the seventeenth in the series of F A Mann Lectures on "Her Majesty's Judges and International Law". Mann warmly acknowledged the debt he owed to Hersch Lauterpacht. He had, he said, an uncanny ability to stimulate, suggest and provoke, and it was his influence that sustained Mann's steadily growing preoccupation

---

[51] This was probably *Judiciary and Executive in Foreign Affairs* (reprinted in *Studies in International Law*, page 391), his first lecture to The Grotius Society, in 1944, and whose subject matter continued to interest him and later led to *Foreign Affairs in English Courts* (1986).

with public international law. But it would be wrong to try to fit Mann into the rather narrow category labelled public international law. His interest lay in the border territory between that law, the Law of Nations whose Father was Grotius and whose subject matter is the customary rules which regulate the intercourse between states; and national systems of law; and the interaction between the two. In the preface to *Studies in International Law* he described them as "certainly distinct branches of the law, yet branches of the same tree."

Lauterpacht was a prophet as well as a scholar and Mann became his disciple. Both believed, over the objections of cynics, that nations could and should subject themselves to a higher law. Moral and legal principles should apply to states as they applied to individuals. This was not mere theory fit for the doctoral thesis or the lecture room. The events of the century in which they both lived had given an urgency to their argument.

Mann wrote much on this subject, showing how international law could be developed by analogy from national legal systems, and how conversely international law could come to form part of those national systems. Lauterpacht, whose seminal work on this theme, *Private Law Sources and Analogies of International Law,* was published in 1927, prompted and encouraged Mann all the time. In a letter written to Mann in 1954, the only one apparently surviving from what must have been a long correspondence, he pointed out that the speech of the Scots Law Lord, Lord Macmillan, in a case on the requisitioning of a ship during the Spanish civil war showed how a change in international law could result in a corresponding change to English law.[52]

---

[52] *The Cristina* [1938] AC 485, 496–7.

Mann's reputation was international to an extent hardly appreciated in England. His writings were and are known and respected throughout Western Europe and beyond. From 1973 he was an active member of the prestigious *Institut de Droit International*, a self-electing body of the great and good in international law from all over the world. His articles and lectures continue to feature in the reading lists which are prepared for the use of the Judges of the International Court in The Hague. He is known for his writings also in the Far East. How well was strikingly illustrated by an incident which occurred during a lecture tour he made from Hong Kong into mainland China towards the end of his life. He visited the old University of Canton. The campus was almost deserted and the effects of the Cultural Revolution were only too evident. But a group of elderly academics had gathered to hear Mann speaking through an interpreter. They sat round the edge of the room drinking tea and listening intently. One of them got up and shuffled out of the room. He returned a few moments later with a book he wanted Mann to see. It was a copy of an early edition of *The Legal Aspect of Money*.

Mann gave two series of lectures at The Hague Academy[53] which Lawrence Collins, whose mentor Mann was, has adjudged his most impressive and lasting achievements apart from The *Legal Aspect of Money*. The subject was in each case jurisdiction, the question of how far a state can claim to affect events or people outside its own territory. Lord Hoffmann acknowledged that reading these lectures had helped him to frame more

---

[53] *The Doctrine of Jurisdiction in International Law:* 111 Hague Recueil (1964) 146; *Studies in International Law* page 1; and *The Doctrine of International Jurisdiction Revisited after 20 Years:* 186 Hague Recueil (1984) 19; *Further Studies in International Law* page 1.

than one judgment, and cited them in a case on whether an American bank should be required to disclose its records in England.[54]   In his writings on international law, as in his book of Money, Mann demonstrated for his English readers the value of drawing on comparative material from other legal systems.   If a sufficiently general acceptance of a rule could be gathered from a comparative survey, a unifying principle would emerge. But he also respected the English belief that legal rules should be more about practical utility than abstractions. How these apparently contradictory tendencies could be reconciled is well illustrated in an article he wrote for the *Law Quarterly Review* in 1959, *Outlines of a History of Expropriation.*[55]   The long-time editor of the Review, Arthur Goodhart, told him that it was the best thing he had ever written.

Mann was a polemicist who wrote like an advocate. It was all of a piece with the way he conducted litigation. The carefully balanced pro and con were not for him; no quarter was asked for or given. In his fearsome critiques of judgments the shaft never failed to go home, but none of the judges seemed to be wounded. This was explained by the courtesy with which he usually framed his language as well as the force and conviction of his argument. He would often write more in sorrow than anger and would speak of a decision as "tragic", as if he were recalling some prelapsarian age, or as if those who had strayed from the true path had shown themselves unworthy of their trust. As he sat in court listening to the argument he watched the judges with an intensity that must have been unnerving. They knew that there was a good chance that

---

[54] *MacKinnon v Donaldson, Lufkin and Jenrette* [1986] Ch. 482, 493.
[55] *75 Law Quarterly Review* (1959) 188.

he was preparing his missile for the next number of the *Law Quarterly Review*.

A selection of Mann's shorter pieces was published posthumously[56]. It contains many of his most trenchant observations. As Lord Neill remarked in his review[57], it is "impossible to read a page without hearing the voice and conjuring up the image of Francis Mann probing, chiding, rebuking, exhorting." A couple of examples will show how true this was.

"There is an air of tragedy about the decision of the House of Lords in Inland Revenue *Commissioners v Rossminster*"[58], he wrote without irony when the Law Lords decided that a tax statute entitled police and inland revenue officials to enter private premises at 7 in the morning and, without giving any detail of what they were searching for, to collect and remove documents of all sorts including children's school reports. There was no subsequent prosecution. Elsewhere he described the result as probably the most regrettable decision of the twentieth century, one which caused more despair than any other known to him. He was affronted that the case was decided without reference to the European Convention on Human Rights. "There is no doubt," he wrote with profound feeling, "that in the light of the experience between 1933 and 1945 the knock at the door at night for unspecified reasons was one of the evils against which the Convention was intended to protect."

---

[56] *Notes and Comments on Cases in International Law, Commercial Law, and Arbitration.* Clarendon Press 1992.

[57] 110 *Law Quarterly Review* (1994) 654.

[58] [1980] 1 All ER 80; *Statutory Interpretation and Human Rights and Fundamental Freedoms:* 96 *Law Quarterly Review* (1980) 201; *Notes and Comments on Cases in International Law, Commercial Law and Arbitration*, p.76.

He much regretted what then seemed to be a growing practice of the Law Lords to deliver only one speech for the whole tribunal, rather than one each, with the remaining four merely concurring, usually in a single sentence. Lord Wilberforce observed (at Mann's memorial event in January 1992) that the English style of discursive judgments presented him with the best possible material on which to deploy his analytical and his critical genius. How much richer the material if there were five, rather than one, such judgments. But he had other reasons for calling the trend towards the single speech "a misfortune"[59]. Law Lords who merely agree with a colleague's opinion "may not necessarily analyse and scrutinise it to the same extent as would be required if they had to write their own opinions ... Perhaps it would not even be regarded as polite to argue about individual phrases or incidental arguments." There were decisions, he wrote, which include sentences that have acquired, but do not necessarily deserve, almost statutory authority: if there is no qualification or differentiation to be found, they are liable to be misunderstood. This could lead to judges being "almost afraid of" stating a clear principle, and avoiding doing so." In a courteous but unmistakable way he was saying that the single speech was lazy and would encourage timidity.

He carried his campaigns to unusual lengths, and would occasionally publish criticisms of the decisions in which the judges had come down against him. After the *Zeiss* case had been lost by his West German clients in the House of Lords in 1967, he wrote a long article under the title, *Germany's Present Legal Status Revisited*[60]. In it

---

[59] *The Single Speech:* 107 *Law Quarterly Review* (1991) 519.

[60] *International and Comparative Law Quarterly* (1967) 760; *Studies in International Law* page 660.

he used the adverse decision in *Zeiss* as a launching pad to review the legal position of Germany and introduced much hostile criticism of the Lords' decision.

The background to the case was that the United Kingdom government did not recognise the government of the German Democratic Republic in East Germany. It disapproved of it. The Russians had set it up in their zone of occupied Germany in breach of the agreement between the four victor powers. So, in answer to a question put to him by the Court of Appeal as a result of an application made by Mann's counsel, the Foreign Secretary stated that, far from recognising the German Democratic Republic as a sovereign state, the United Kingdom government recognised only the Soviet Union as entitled to exercise governing authority in its zone of Germany.

If the government does not recognise a foreign entity as a sovereign state the courts must follow suit. This meant that in law the German Democratic Republic did not exist. None of the laws it purported to make could have any effect in the United Kingdom. The Court of Appeal had accepted these stark consequences and decided that, because the East German *Zeiss* was an agency of the German Democratic Republic, its proceedings against the West German *Zeiss* must be struck out. But it seemed to the House of Lords that to treat East Germany as if it did not exist would be to fly in the face of the facts. So they found a way of giving effect to East German laws and so saving the proceedings. They decided that the Soviet Union, being the sovereign or governing authority in the Russian zone, had set up the German Democratic Republic as a dependent or subordinate organisation. Sir Robert Jennings described this solution as "a bold if unconvincing application of the notion of agency to governments"; but it enabled the Lords to reach the conclusion that the East German Zeiss company had been established under an authority recognised by the United Kingdom, and so could sue in the English courts.

Mann was very unhappy. He felt that this was an intellectually dishonest way out of the difficulty caused by the undoubted fact that the United Kingdom government had not recognised the German Democratic Republic. He said as much in his article, *The Present Legal Status of Germany Revisited*, deploying a closely reasoned argument supported by material from other jurisdictions. Later on he went further in his book, *Foreign Affairs in English Courts* (1986), describing the decision as resting on "a false, indeed a fictitious basis". Lord Upjohn, he said, "gave the show away" by describing the consequences of non-recognition as too deplorable to contemplate for "any highly civilised community with which we have substantial trading relationships ... unless the law compels that conclusion". Mann thought the law did compel that conclusion, and that the Lords had decided as they did for political reasons. To allow political considerations to influence a judgment was a slippery slope at the bottom of which lay the perversion of justice.

Zeiss was a rare but not the only example of writing by what some took to be a disappointed litigant[61]. But Mann would not admit the charge of sour grapes. He felt his extra knowledge of the case entitled him to

[61] For example, *The Protection of Shareholders' Interests in the light of the* Barcelona Traction *Case*: 67 *American Journal of International Law* (1973) 259; *Further Studies in International Law* page 217. For another striking instance, see a Note by Mann in 102 *Law Quarterly Review* (1968) 191; and Collins: *Dr F A Mann: His Work and Influence:* 1993 British Year Book of International Law, 92, 93.

publish his views when a really serious miscarriage of justice had occurred. Lord Wilberforce, one of the Law Lords who had disappointed Mann in the *Zeiss* case, did not disapprove of Mann's riposte. He appreciated the disputation.

Mann's writings were profoundly scholarly. His thinking was original and always expressed with a view to the practical consequences of the propositions he was putting forward. His command of comparative material illuminated his studies, above all his treatise on the law of money, and added force to his argument. This resource was derived from the traditions of German scholarship. The scope and number of his writings were extraordinary. A *Festschrift*, containing essays in both German and English was published in Germany for his 70th birthday. It contained a list of some 400 of his writings. That was in 1977. Many more were published in the 14 years remaining. He had always intended to go on to the end. In the same year, 1977, a series of annual lectures was established in his honour by his partners and a group of friends, and at the dinner after the first in the series, given by Lord Diplock, he quoted one of his heroes, Oliver Wendell Holmes. He recalled that the great judge was himself honoured with the Theodore Roosevelt Medal when he was 83 and was still a member of the Supreme Court of the United States. Holmes had made a short simple speech for the occasion. "For five minutes", he said, "you made the dream of a life seem true. But one who is still in the firing line cannot dream long. I hope that the short time that is left to me will not dim the honour of today." Mann, who also intended to stay in the firing line, said that he had nothing to add.

He took pleasure from his study and his writing. He used to say that he would get more satisfaction from *nn*

good page of fiction than from all of his legal
d he knew well the cramped formal style in
as necessary to cast his speculations and his
scholarship. Nevertheless it had its own satisfaction, and
he chose a phrase from the letters of the younger Pliny to
head the preface to his *Studies in International Law*.

Porro ut ex studiis gaudium sic studia hilaritate proveniunt.

If one's work is to give pleasure it must have its inspiration
in happiness.

VIII

Legal Practice

Personal independence was the thing that Francis Mann prized above everything. This was as true of his attitude to his professional practice as it was of his writings. He could not understand how anyone with the good fortune and wit to choose, could prefer the life of a civil servant or become an executive in a large business, rather than pursue a profession. His fear for the city solicitors' firms, with one of which, Herbert Smith, he made his life from 1958 until his death, was that they would become "institutionalised" and too like a big corporation. Bureaucracy with its layers of management, he considered, would stifle initiative and introduce temptations to conform and comply. It would conflict directly with independence, which he defined as following your own judgement, applying your own standards and, above all, retaining the moral courage to say no. No one who knew him could say that he fell short of that definition in anything that he did himself.

He had not wanted to become a solicitor. It was forced on him by the exigencies of his early life in England. He would have preferred the Bar; but by the time he could have afforded to make the change, and had realised that his German accent would not have mattered much for the type of case he was undertaking, it was too late. It would, he felt, have been unfair to his partners, and in any case the natural indecisiveness to which he confessed about his own affairs made him leave things as they were.

He was a great admirer of the English system, and in particular of the divided profession. When fusion of the two sides was in the air, he vigorously defended the status quo, and wrote an article for the Law Quarterly Review entitled *Fusion of the Legal Professions?*[62] He explained that he had originally been in favour of merging the solicitors' profession with the Bar, but had come to realise that to do so would threaten the English system of administering justice. At the root of his argument lay the low opinion which he had of solicitors in general and his scepticism about their capacity, except in a few instances, to conduct cases in court. He considered that the English way of trying cases was simply the best in the world – its oral method in which, like a bell that is struck repeatedly to see if it is sound, the advocate's propositions are tested by a sceptical court; the judge coming to the trial with a mind as blank as a sheet of paper, uninfluenced by reading about the case beforehand; and the method of cross examination in which the advocate explores the truth through a wide-ranging and often distinctly uncivil open debate with the witness. To sit with him in court was to see how much he loved these things.

Such a system should not be tampered with. The profession, he was now convinced, must remain divided into barristers and solicitors, each confined to their separate spheres. Others might criticise it as cumbersome, ritualistic and expensive. Maybe, but once allow all lawyers to have rights of audience in court or dilute the tiny Bar which enjoys the confidence of the judges, and the administration of justice itself must be the sufferer.

[62] 93 *Law Quarterly Review* (1977) 367.

He wrote again when there were new proposals to save judges' time by giving advance warning in writing to the court of the arguments which were going to be deployed at the trial. This, it was said, would cut down the time taken by the oral process in which everything had to be read out, and so economise on "judge-power" – a neologism that would have made his hair stand on end. Mann attacked these ideas as dangerous, saying that they would tend to assimilate English procedure to the American and continental models. It was not necessary to elaborate on that horror.[63] Lord Denning, who was perhaps the greatest exponent of managing a traditional hearing with speed and courtesy, applauded, and wrote a personal note (20 June 1984).

> I believe so whole-heartedly about *oral* argument – I did not read the papers beforehand – so as not to pre-judge the case … Your article ought to have a lot of effect – but in the present climate I feel it will not. But, dear Francis, we do value all you do – and admire all you have done in your great career.

So he became and remained a solicitor. One of the compensations which he discovered was that a solicitor is closer to his client than a barrister, and he was able to indulge his natural curiosity about the vagaries of human nature. He advised some notables: Somerset Maugham, Armand Hammer, the Chairman of Occidental Petroleum and a maverick figure in the world of east-west relations, and Nubar Gulbenkian. It is a pity that he left no written sketches of these personalities, except for a short account of Gulbenkian, for whom he acted over a period of some fifteen years. Gulbenkian's affairs exemplified the tenacity and stubborn unwillingness to

---

[63] *Reflections on English Civil Justice and the Rule of Law:* Civil Justice Quarterly (1983) 320.

compromise which characterise family disputes. Nubar was the son of Calouste Gulbenkian, the celebrated "Mr 5 per cent" of the oil industry. His obsession was to get his own back on his father with whom he had enjoyed an intense love-hate relationship until Calouste's death in 1956. Thereafter the vendetta was pursued against the family trustees in an elaborately barbed correspondence. The antagonists included Charles Whishaw, the urbane senior partner of the solicitors, Freshfields, and Lord Radcliffe, whom Mann described as "a man of unusual intelligence and perspicacity, but at the same time one of the coldest and most remote men I ever met". Nubar himself, he thought, was "a man of some quality, albeit without depth." Amusing and kindly but interested, it seemed, only in horses and high society; he was a snob in the world class and enlivened the trials of his cases by providing fabulous cold collations for his lawyers during the lunch adjournments. Mann much enjoyed acting for him.

Although he engaged his clients' interests with the utmost dedication, he also liked to be amused. This could sometimes extend to the macabre. Mann's friend, George Weidenfeld, published a book by a former senior Nazi in which a named woman was depicted as a high-class prostitute and double agent. She sued for libel. The only way to get her to come to the table to compromise her enormous claim seemed to be by pleading justification, that is to assert that all the allegations were true. So Weidenfeld and Mann travelled to Salzburg and interviewed a number of former ranking SS officers. Mann recalled dining with these people and humouring them to obtain their evidence. They were naturally at pains to assure their Jewish interlocutors that they knew nothing of the atrocities for which the SS was a byword. The case was duly settled, and Mann described the experience with barely credible understatement as "rather a paradoxical situation".

The camaraderie of the profession was very congenial to Mann. He drew most of his friends from the Bench and Bar, those with whom he had worked and fought cases. His closest were Michael Kerr and Mark Littman, with whom he took regular Sunday morning walks in Kensington Gardens. Kerr's father, Alfred Kerr, was the celebrated critic and man of letters who was living in Berlin while Mann was there, and whom Richard Mann had known. The Sunday walks were a legend, and it was disappointing to those who thought that abstruse concepts of jurisprudence were aired beside the Round Pond to learn that Mann considered that his two friends, although advocates of the very first rank, were not interested in theory. He was fascinated by the way in which barristers treated the obligation of confidence which they owed to clients. They gossiped endlessly but somehow never seemed to betray a secret that mattered. Even the judges talked about pending cases to him.

On one occasion he had lost a case before Lord Denning and discussed it with him afterwards. "There was no merit in your man's case", said Denning. Mann argued with him and said that if all cases were decided simply by the criterion of which party was the more deserving, the law would be a lie. In any event, Mann suggested, it would be wrong to decide a case on "merit" alone without hearing argument on the pros and cons of that issue; but this was not allowed because it would be said to be irrelevant. The great man had his answer. "We see through all that – we do not need an argument on merit." If Otto Kahn-Freund had heard that exchange, he would surely have felt richly justified in the remark he made in a letter to Mann that English law is not really teachable because it is inarticulate.

The conversation between Mann and Denning approached the central paradox of Denning's career on the Bench. How could he be a great English judge, perhaps the greatest of the twentieth century, when he could, if occasion demanded, play fast and loose with the rules of the game, the sanctity of precedent and the hierarchy of the appeal system? Mann's view was that all British lawyers owed Denning a debt of gratitude. He was the only real stimulator on the Bench and kept the law on the move. "If we never do anything which has not been done before", he had said, "we shall never get anywhere. The law will stand still whilst the rest of the world goes on: and that will be bad for both."[64] Few judges had done more to remove the shackles of obsolete rules; or to create an effective administrative law by which the judges could exert some control over the executive; or to stand up to those over-mighty subjects, the trade unions. There was, Mann thought, a moral purpose in all Denning did, and his perception of where the law ought to be going was sound. He knew of course that the means Denning employed to achieve his ends were sometimes questionable. That ineffable charm and Hampshire burr, the simple transparent prose, masked his ruthlessness. So what if someone whose purposes fell short of Denning's high-minded ends should try to emulate him? Mann recognised the peril. But it was enough that the great man whose friendship he had earned was achieving single-handedly so much that was good. Others abide our question. Thou art free.

[64] *Packer v Packer* [1954] P. 15, 22.

Mann believed that in most cases at the end of a hearing the judge stands back and asks himself who deserves to win. This is not merely a matter of "feel" or hunch: it is also based on experience. A judge may not even be fully conscious of the process that he is going through. He acknowledged that this might sound cynical, but it had to be accepted as a fact of life. It was a fact which he deplored because it tended to arbitrariness in decision making. That however was no reason to pretend that it did not exist. He always drew his students' attention to it. It was something that must be understood and tackled. "How do we get rid of an attitude of mind," he wrote, "which, if followed by lesser men than Lord Denning, constitutes a great danger?"

There is a lot to advocacy beyond knowing and expounding the case in an orderly way. Mann greatly enjoyed putting to use the tricks of the trade. There was the case of Mr. Gompertz. He and his cousin, Mr. Meinrath, both of whom were Jewish, had been equal partners in a button factory in Germany before the war. Meinrath came to England and set up a similar business, again with Gompertz as equal shareholder. Gompertz was trapped in Belgium and spent the period of the German occupation hiding in a cellar. When it was over he wrote to Meinrath a pathetic letter asking for his shares and the dividends which had accrued, saying that he had nothing left in the world. He received by way of reply a letter from solicitors. Your reference to shares is not understood, they said, you do not own any shares in Gompertz & Meinrath, nor are any dividends held for your account. By some means Gompertz' shares had been transferred into the names of associates of Meinrath. Mann instructed Valentine Holmes KC and J G Strangman for Gompertz, presumably on legal aid. Holmes opened the case on a

Monday morning. At about 12.45 he reached the letter from Gompertz and read it out to the judge slowly, without emphasis or comment. The answer is on the next page, he said, and then read that out in the same flat way. Then he fell silent. For what seemed like an eternity no one spoke. Through the silence the judge's face became redder. He finally broke the tension and said, "I adjourn now to two o'clock." The parties left the court and just before the resumption Holmes was informed that Meinrath wanted to come to terms.

Mann called the case advocacy by silence. The two counsel, Valentine Holmes and Tom Strangman, were favourites of his. Both personified the idiosyncratic spirit of independence which could be found in the Temple and Lincoln's Inn, and which Mann so admired. Holmes was an Irishman from Dublin who used to go dog racing with his clerk of an evening. His style in court was diffident but the argument was concise and directed by superb judgement. His knowledge of the court procedure, which was still Dickensian, and its forbidding handbook, the Annual Practice, was legendary. He knew that a high proportion of cases are won before ever they get into court and Mann learned much from him about this abstruse but essential art.

Strangman won seventeen consecutive cases in his partnership with Mann. He was a craggy character and fearsome cross-examiner, but it was his dedication that Mann particularly admired. He proved by example that an advocate must give the case his undivided attention and know it so intimately that in the heat of the moment in a trial he can appreciate, find and exploit the crucial point. Far too many members of the Bar, Mann wrote, believe that they can simultaneously have their fingers in several pies. "The truth is that nobody can and that the hubris of many a fashionable silk has cost his client dearly." To visit Strangman for a conference was a journey into the past. He sat in a grim Victorian room in Lincoln's Inn, slumped in his battered leather chair by the dying embers of the fire, twisting pink string round his finger. He shook his head in pessimistic incredulity at the obstacles presented by the case and the implausibility of the propositions he was supposed to expound. Strangman was used to dominating a conference and was a difficult man to argue with. Even Mann was sometimes reduced to silence and the discussion could reach an impasse. In such cases a drink between the two of them in a nearby bar might then be the last possibility of dissolving the obstruction. But Strangman knew more about the case than anyone and was only rehearsing in his mind what might be said against him in court. He retired to grow orchids in the country and forget about the law; but, Mann wrote, I have not forgotten a great master of the law in practice.

A barrister briefed by Mann was in for a most unusual experience. All who had worked with him agreed that his versatility and learning were prodigious. He was singularly forceful and tenacious, and in a time when the junior branch of the profession (as it was then often spoken of) was deferential to the Bar, he did not defer and he had ideas of his own about how the case should be conducted.

In *Broome v Cassell*,[65] he acted for the publishers of David Irving's book "The Destruction of Convoy PQ17". The subject was one of the great naval disasters of the second world war and the story is dramatically told in Lord Denning's judgment in the Court of Appeal.[66]

---

[65] [1972] AC 1027.
[66] [1971] 2 QB 354, 371.

Captain Broome had commanded the close escort of destroyers and was a naval officer of unquestioned bravery. The book suggested without any foundation that he had deserted the convoy, leaving it to scatter and fend for itself. Those responsible were far away in the Admiralty. Broome claimed that he had been libelled and was awarded both compensatory and punitive damages. The hearing in the House of Lords was unruly. There were constant interruptions from a full court of seven presided over by the peculiarly loquacious Lord Chancellor, Lord Hailsham. The task of persuading the court that there was something to say for publishers who had wilfully libelled an English naval officer seemed superhuman. But eventually Roger Parker QC, for the publishers, did get a quiet hearing. On the question of damages, the appeal was concerned only with the "punitive" or "exemplary" element and the award was upheld by the narrowest of margins, 4 to 3.

The publishers were ordered to pay Broome's costs. Most of the hearing, however, had been taken up with a debate about the precise circumstances in which damages can be awarded as punishment, as distinct from compensation. This was a technical matter on which the publishers' arguments eventually prevailed.

When Mann had had the opportunity to read the judgments carefully he realised that it was unfair for the publishers to have to pay all the costs. His counsel, Roger Parker and Robert Alexander, while agreeing, were sceptical that any more could be done. The hearing was finished, judgment had been given and the order for costs had been made. The case was over. But Mann was not convinced. He never gave up and he looked into it further. He discovered that the Lords could always vary one of their own orders. At last in this case he had the

merits on his side. He felt it was worth a try. Eventually
he persuaded counsel to put in another petition. At the
resumed hearing Parker put the argument very strongly.
The Law Lords were unexpectedly sympathetic, perhaps
because the main decision had been so touch-and-go, and
the costs order was varied so that the publishers paid half
instead of all of Captain Broome's costs.[67]

Impressions of what Mann was like as a litigating
solicitor from the point of view of the Bar varied. All
admired his learning, dedication and resourcefulness;
all, particularly his opponents, felt the ferocity with
which he pursued the enemy. But some felt that his zeal
interfered with an objective view of the case and that some
of his suggestions were unsound. Michael Kerr thought
that Mann saw every case as a crusade and that somehow
the infidel was always on the other side. He was adept
at uncovering some crucial fact or document, usually of
a sort which reflected discredit on the other side, and
which preferably pointed at fraud. Other advocates,
particularly the more conservative-minded, were
reluctant to advance propositions that might seem *outré*
in court. They felt that they might lose the confidence of
the judge. It was a respectable point of view but Mann,
who often did want to put forward something unusual,
or even at first blush implausible, was impatient with it.
Mark Littman said that he supposed he was more willing
than some to take "far-out" points, and he recalled that
there were "dangerous thoughts" about cases that Mann
did not want counsel to harbour. Whichever way it was
put, Mann felt that a case was a campaign which it was
the General's business to win.

[67] *Broome v Cassell (No. 2)* [1972] AC 1136.

One episode in the *Zeiss* litigation, discussed in the last chapter, is a good illustration of the lengths to which Mann was prepared to go in determination and crusading zeal. No one knew anything about it until ten years after Mann's death when it was uncovered by Lawrence Collins in his researches while preparing his 25th F A Mann lecture given in 2001.[68]

It will be recalled that the West German Zeiss, for whom Mann was acting, had applied to strike out proceedings begun by the East German Zeiss on the ground that the East German company had no standing to sue in England because it was incorporated under the law of a state (the German Democratic Republic in east Germany) that the United Kingdom did not recognise. The Court of Appeal decided in favour of the West German Zeiss; the East Germans appealed to the House of Lords. The hearing in the Lords went badly for Mann. It became clear from the dialogue with counsel that the Law Lords were seeking ways to avoid the extreme consequences of the Court of Appeal's decision.

It seems that after the hearing in the Lords but before judgment was given Mann decided, on his own initiative and without consulting anyone else, to try to enlist the government's help. In the evening of 15 December 1965 he called on Mr J L Simpson of the Legal Adviser's department of the Foreign Office. According to documents in the Foreign Office records, he told Mr Simpson that the Law Lords seemed to be against his clients on the question of recognition of East Germany, and were therefore likely to decide that East German law should

---

[68] For the revised text of the lecture see: *Foreign Relations and the Judiciary:* 51 *International and Comparative Law Quarterly* (2002) 485.

be given effect in England. He left a note of some further questions which it was proposed to move the House of Lords the next day to address to the Foreign Secretary. In the event the House refused the motion on 16 December. Mann paid a second visit to Mr Simpson that evening and said, in effect, that all was lost from the West German Zeiss point of view, and that they and their legal advisers wanted any help they could get from the Foreign Office. He indicated how he thought the Lords would decide the case, and urged that an intervention by the Law Officers at this eleventh hour should be considered.

Mr Simpson thought the legal arguments for and against intervention were "finely balanced". If the House of Lords were to reach a conclusion on the lines forecast by Dr Mann, he asked, "Would this be disagreeable from our point of view ... ?" The response to this pregnant question was not found in the files, but it is to be inferred that the Foreign Office found it convenient to do nothing. In any event no attempt was made by the government to deflect the House of Lords from reaching their expected conclusion that East Germany was a puppet of the Soviet Union. That conclusion would not be inconsistent with the principle that the UK did not recognise the German Democratic Republic, while preserving the valuable trading relationship between Britain and East Germany.

The whole episode was completely unknown to Mann's Counsel, Michael Kerr and Mark Littman, until it was revealed in Lord Collins' lecture. Although they were his two closest friends at the Bar, he felt that there were some things that even counsel should not know.

Lord Wilberforce, who had a long experience of working with Mann before he went to the Bench in 1961 and who was a lifelong admirer, saw it differently. He thought that Mann was unique. He reversed the normal roles of solicitor and barrister: Mann was the expert, and counsel became the generalist whose task it was to convert Mann's work into an argument suitable for an English judge. For Mann there was a point of principle in every case which the argument would elucidate and lead to. It was like revealing a mystery. In his memorial tribute to Mann he elaborated this view:

> When a dispute arises, there is an unstructured mess of facts, hundreds of documents – known and potential – many incipient points of law and arguments. Francis would start at once to structure them, to build up a factual and legal composition with, at the top, some interesting and fundamental point of law, which he alone understood and of whose rightness he would be convinced – rather like the process by which we are told life originated from an unorganised slime under the influence of organising radiation.

This style or working method of Mann's, although it should not be labelled as "characteristically German", was, thought Lord Wilberforce, foreign to the traditionally pragmatic English way: and that was possibly why he, Lord Wilberforce, and other judges in England often disappointed Mann. It was easier for counsel to use his method in argument than for judges to accept it.

Knowing what Francis Mann achieved, it is easy to forget the humble beginnings of his English professional life. At first he was able to advise, and appear as an expert witness, only on German law. By degrees he began to handle English work as an unadmitted clerk, and then as an articled clerk just before the war. During the war he was still unqualified but he was in fact running the practice of Swann, Hardman while Douglas Phillips was serving in the army. Only after he returned from Berlin in late 1946 did he lay the foundations of his reputation as an outstanding practitioner. The earliest cases were about refugee problems; what they faced in their new lives in England and the consequences of their exile from Germany. Much of it was an attempt to undo the work of the Nazis. Within a few months of arriving he learned how, in the English tradition of an oral trial, it was possible to lose a case in the first few minutes.

Mr Graham Maw, the senior partner of a well-known solicitors' firm who became a staunch supporter, consulted him on behalf of Dr. Sommer, a Jewish industrialist from Dresden who had insured his property on Lloyd's against the risk of loss from requisition or confiscation by the German government. Shortly after Hitler came to power and while Dr. Sommer was abroad, thugs in the uniform of the SA occupied his premises to set up a so-called "corruption bureau". At the trial of the claim against Lloyd's he was represented by Mr Stuart Bevan KC, Mr D N Pritt KC and Mr Hubert Parker, the future Lord Chief Justice. Bevan opened the case by explaining that some people called "storm troopers" had taken possession of Dr. Sommer's house, drunk his wine, slept in his bed and generally made free with his things. The judge thereupon remarked that the case did not seem to be about "loss" at all; it looked like a clear case of trespass. From this setback the plaintiff never recovered and the claim failed.[69]

It was a salutary lesson. An incautious remark by counsel might put a kink in a case which could never be straightened out. And the *Sommer* case and others like it showed Mann how difficult it would be to make judges and barristers, a fairly representative group of conservative middle class men, understand the true

[69] *Sommer v Matthews* 49 L1. LR (1934) 154.

nature of Nazism until it was forced into their minds by the war. "You must not try to inflame my mind too much ....", said the judge at one point in the opening. "After all, we are not trying the Nazi Government." Mann never forgot a moral like the one he had had in that case.

He learned other things too: the approach to foreign law of the English legal mind. There was a tendency to uphold the lawgiver, whoever he might be, and a disinclination to enquire about the character or provenance of law made outside England. This was due partly to the English political scene in which lawyers had been brought up, where parliament was supreme and it was the judges' part to interpret the statute and no more. They had no experience of acting as a constitutional court. As has been seen, Mann wrote about the shortcomings of this tendency when he advocated a Bill of Rights for Britain.

But more importantly, the judges were cautious when they spoke *ex cathedra* about the validity and consequences of foreign law. The law of another country was to be proved as a fact like any other piece of evidence, and when proved was to be accepted and adopted. There were few exceptions to this rule and there was a belief in restraint. Where might it end if they were saying this law was good and this bad? In general of course Mann accepted this as a healthy tendency. But surely it was different if the courts were faced with the legal consequences of Nazism? And because his cases were concerned with the problems of German refugees, the question came up repeatedly.

One such case was tried in 1950 and was about the well-known music publishing business of C F Peters of Leipzig.[70] The owners were a Jewish family, Henri

---

[70] *Novello v Hinrichsen* [1951] 1 Ch. 595.

Hinrichsen and his son Hans, both of whom were incarcerated in a concentration camp in 1938. In that year a series of Nazi decrees were made giving power to the Ministry of Propaganda to confiscate Jewish businesses. A "trustee" was appointed under these powers and he sold the business at a gross undervalue to nominees of Hermann Goering. The Hinrichsens were released and required to leave Germany at once. They went to live in Belgium where they both died during the war, as Mann believed, having been murdered by the Nazis. Novello claimed to be entitled to exploit the UK copyrights by virtue of a licence granted to them under wartime emergency legislation. They sued Max Hinrichsen, a surviving son of the family who had managed to escape to England, for infringement of copyright. He contended that the "sale" to Goering's puppets was not valid and ought not to be given effect in England; and that therefore he had inherited the copyrights from his father and brother. Mann was retained as an expert witness for him.

At the time of the trial there were conflicting decisions of the German courts about whether transactions like the "sale" of the Peters business – and there were many – were valid or not. Mann was in the witness box for six days. His evidence was that all such contracts were fatally tainted according to German law. For Novello, Mr E J Cohn gave evidence that the sale was valid. The judge, Mr Justice Wynn-Parry, preferred Cohn's view. Mann's later recollection of the case is worth quoting:

> In the result the Judge could not be persuaded to adopt a view so inconsistent with the positivistic approach and literalism so characteristic of and traditional for an English lawyer – there are no more positivistic lawyers anywhere than in England. He felt that logic required him to hold the [sale] contract valid. Nevertheless it was of course clear

that he would not decide in favour of a defendant who presented so undeserving a case. He held that the contract was in substance confiscatory and could not therefore have extra-territorial effect so as to dispose of the non-German copyrights.[71]

That tells much about the English judicial mind, as Francis Mann saw it. Admirer though he was of the system and its judges, that never was a reason why they should be immune from his criticism. He considered that many of them preferred not to tackle problems frontally and would rather find a more roundabout or even "fudged" way of meeting the merits of the case. To do justice by practical expedient, Mann perceived once more, was thought better than establishing a principle.

Later events in Germany vindicated Mann's opinion in the *Hinrichsen* case. The Federal Supreme Court developed its concept of a "pure" or fundamental law which no dictator or other legislator could displace. Arbitrary or oppressive laws which were contrary to this fundamental law were perversions. They were *unrecht* or "non-law". This was the foundation for later decisions that treated as illegal those acts that Nazi laws had sanctioned, as Mann explained in his writings.[72] He considered this development to be one of the greatest achievements of the Court; and it was one that agreed closely with his own conception of fundamental law.

The *Hinrichsen* case had an unusual importance for Mann's career. The judge, Mr Justice Wynn-Parry, was appointed Chairman of the Lord Chancellor's Committee

---

[71] It is an established principle that English courts will not recognise a law of a foreign state confiscating property outside its own territory.

[72] *The Present Validity of Nazi Nationality Laws:* 89 Law Quarterly Review (1973) 194, 199.

on Private International Law two years after the trial; and Mann always believed that it was because he had been an expert witness in the case that he was himself appointed a member of the committee. It sat between 1952 and 1964 when, although it had done useful work, it was allowed to die without explanation. These were important years for Mann's growing practice, and work on the Committee led to useful contacts. Mann met many who were or were to become judges.

He was also a member of the Council of the British Institute of International and Comparative Law from its inception in 1958. This was a merger of two other academic bodies, the Grotius Society and the Society of Comparative Legislation. The two were very different. The Grotius Society was set up in 1915 by a group of academics, judges and senior civil servants. Their purpose, formed in the midst of a world war, was to encourage the resolution of disputes between states by peaceful means and in accordance with the conventions of international law. The Society of Comparative Legislation was formed in 1894 by lawyers in the civil service from Britain and the Commonwealth. Its object was to keep the common law harmonious throughout the Commonwealth, an ideal which was close to Lord Denning's heart. He was the chairman of its executive committee from 1951. Whereas Mann joined the Grotius only in 1946, probably because its membership was restricted to British subjects and he had to wait until then for naturalisation, he had joined the Society of Comparative Legislation as early as 1934, within a year of coming to Britain. He was interested in academic work of this more practical type and membership of these bodies gave him an *entrée* into circles which were bound to be congenial. It did something to counteract the loneliness of his academic life. The contacts were valuable as well. Among the names of the subscribers to the constitution of the British Institute were Lord Denning, Lord McNair, Hartley Shawcross, Geoffrey Cheshire, Richard Wilberforce, Hersch Lauterpacht and Kenneth Diplock. But it was Denning who was the prime mover in joining the work of these two bodies and who was the President of the British Institute from its birth until 1986. The friendship between Mann and Denning owed much to the work they did together there. The British Institute published the respected International and Comparative Law Quarterly and was housed in the same building as the Institute of Advanced Legal Studies. It was there, in the library in Russell Square, that Mann spent most of his Saturdays.

The *Hinrichsen* case had another and, for Mann, more important aspect. It was its jurisprudence which really touched him. He felt that he was part of a crusade to outlaw the legacy of Nazism. All men of goodwill ought to join. He could not understand how his opponent E J Cohn, who was himself a refugee and a Jew, could take the other side and support an insupportable transaction or defend the validity of ideas which had caused misery to so many. Mann was convinced that in his heart Cohn felt as he did. In a sense all Mann's cases were crusades. There was a passion in him which made it so. It did not follow of course that he deprecated all those who acted on the other side. But when it came to this central theme – should effect be given to Nazi laws – a case could not be treated as if it were just another point of law to be legitimately debated on one side or the other. The theme recurred through his professional life, culminating in his decisive intervention in the extraordinary case of *Oppenheimer v Cattermole*, discussed above.

The defeat of Germany in 1945 brought Mann a flood of work for refugees and other nationals of foreign countries that he could now deal with as a qualified solicitor. The Custodian of Enemy Property was winding up his affairs. He was the government official who had taken control of all property owned by enemy nationals, a term that included not only Germans but also nationals of the occupied European countries. The policy of the government was generous. It proposed not only to restore the property of those who had been victims of Nazi oppression, but also those who throughout the war had escaped the terror and lived outside enemy territory. Mann recalled that he had literally hundreds of these cases.

One case about enemy property dwarfed all others, *Bank voor Handel en Scheepvaart v Slatford*.[73] In 1947, shortly after Mann had returned from Berlin, John Foster introduced him to Henry Hyde, a New York lawyer whom Foster had met when he was First Secretary in the Washington embassy. Hyde was looking for a London solicitor to deal with the multifarious affairs of Baron Heini Thyssen, the nephew of the German coal and steel magnate and whose father had married a Hungarian noblewoman and taken Hungarian nationality. The Baron, himself a man of vast wealth, lived in Lugano and was also a Hungarian national. In this way Mann came to act in the Baron's interest, a connection which kept him occupied, particularly with the Baron's matrimonial affairs, over a large part of the rest of his career.

Baron Thyssen was the controlling shareholder of a Dutch bank which at the outbreak of war in 1939 owned a quantity of gold in a safe deposit in London. When the Netherlands were overrun in 1940 the bank became

[73] [1953] 1 QB 248.

an enemy national. The Dutch government, which was in exile in London, made a decree seizing all property belonging to anyone who was resident in the occupied Netherlands. It included the gold bars. The purpose of the seizure was to prevent the property from falling into the hands of the Germans. But shortly after the Dutch decree was made the gold was vested in the Custodian of Enemy Property under the Trading with the Enemy legislation, and he sold it. There was therefore a conflict between the decree of the Dutch government and the seizure by the Custodian. Who owned the gold or its sale proceeds, the bank, the Dutch government or the Baron? To whom should the Custodian look?   If the owner was the Baron it would have been normal for the Custodian to transfer it to him since he had been living in Switzerland outside enemy territory throughout the war.   But the British government was suspicious of the name Thyssen. They suspected some connection with the vast industrial interests of the family in the Ruhr basin which had been such a vital part of the German war machine. The Dutch government too took a keen interest in the outcome of the case and Mann had to confer constantly with them.

Mark Littman, who had been Foster's pupil and whose first big case this was, recalled that Mann, representing the bank, conducted an adroit campaign in correspondence with the Custodian. He allowed that official to believe that the true owner of the gold was not the bank but the Baron as controlling shareholder. This was contrary to all principle. Nonetheless, the Custodian did hold that view, and because the Baron was Hungarian he considered, without discouragement from Mann, that he should transfer the sale proceeds of the gold to the official concerned with the distribution of Hungarian enemy property under the peace treaty with Hungary.

This having been done, the bank sued both the Custodian for having wrongfully parted with the money, and the Administrator of Hungarian Property for the sale price of the gold.

Mann retained Sir Walter Monckton KC to lead John Foster, then a young silk, and Mark Littman. On the other side for the Crown was a formidable team: the Solicitor-General, Sir Lynn Ungoed-Thomas KC, with Mr Gerald Upjohn KC, Mr J P Ashworth and Mr Roger Parker, all future members of the higher judiciary. Monckton was not a profound lawyer and he needed a good deal of help. But he had a silver tongue and he knew people in high places. He displayed these assets early. It was, as Mann now learned and later put to use, sometimes possible to "arrange" which judge should hear a particular case. In spite of the horror always shown by Mann's German students when he explained it to them, this was neither bribery nor corruption. It was simply an empiric rule at work, according to which it is recognised that there are "horses for courses". Monckton telephoned Sir Hartley Shawcross, the Attorney-General, in Mann's presence, and asked him to whom he thought they should entrust this important case. Shawcross asked for suggestions. Monckton proposed three names. Which is your own choice? asked Shawcross. Monckton replied: (Sir Patrick) Devlin. Shawcross at once agreed. Mann was quite certain that on both sides quality was the only criterion.

It was a striking example of something that he always emphasised. All judges are in theory equal, but in fact they are not. The lawyer who practises in the courts must know his judges. There may be an opportunity like this one to choose, but in any event the litigant should be forewarned of the idiosyncracies of the tribunal that he has to face.

Mann considered that Devlin had one of the finest intellects that ever adorned the English bench; and Monckton would certainly not have been able to conduct a sustained debate with him, unaided. He had to be "crammed" and buoyed up with notes from John Foster, Mark Littman and from Mann on every conceivable contingency to which Devlin's penetrating mind might lead. It was a demanding task with not a little anxiety. In the result, however, Devlin decided in favour of the bank and gave a judgment of notable lucidity and compression.[74] He ruled that, because the gold bars were an asset which was outside Dutch jurisdiction, the decree of the Dutch government was not effective to transfer ownership to itself, even though it was the act of a friendly government taken in its own and British interests; that the gold was properly vested in the Custodian of Enemy Property; and that it was the bank itself and not its Hungarian shareholder which was entitled to the sale proceeds. The victory was an early milestone in Mann's career as a litigating solicitor.

During the first ten years after the war Mann's primary concern was to build his practice in partnership with Douglas Phillips in the re-named firm of Hardman, Phillips and Mann. Even his writing was subordinated. By the spring of 1955 he reckoned that a solid base had been laid down. Phillips was then 55 and Mann 47. Both could look forward to many years of co-operation, Phillips in family practice and Mann in international and commercial work. This future was blown away by Phillips' untimely death in a motor cycle accident. Mann

---

[74] For a discussion of the case and its importance in international law, see Lawrence Collins: *Dr F A Mann: His Work and Influence.* British Year Book of International Law 1993, page 65.

lost the colleague who had done more than anyone to help him start and who was in his own words, "a faithful and warm-hearted friend, an intelligent colleague imbued with common sense, but also with enthusiasm and energy." He was consumed with grief, and deeply worried about how the practice was now to be carried on. Fortunately help came in the summer of 1957. Through the intermediacy of his friend Hans Frank, whom he had known in pre-Hitler Berlin and was now a New York lawyer, and a remarkable accountant, Joe Smith of Cooper Brothers, who had never qualified but knew everyone of consequence in the City, arrangements were made for the merger of Mann's firm with the city practice of Herbert Smith & Co.

It took effect from the beginning of 1958. Mann and his young partner, Derek Spottiswoode, joined the City partnership. It was a happy and fruitful union. For Mann, it meant that he now had the resources of a firm of high repute with nine partners and a staff of about sixty, and could recruit younger lawyers to help him handle the bigger cases. His anxieties about money eased. His wife recalled that he had often used to say in the early days: "My practice is dead, we shall starve in the gutter"; but that after he joined Herbert Smith he left out the second half of the lament. For the firm, it meant that the horizon widened. In common with the other large City firms, the practice was growing fast but was still narrowly based on financial work within the square mile. The outlook was insular. The litigation practice which was to grow into one of international reputation was still in 1958 in an early phase. Until a few years earlier "contentious business", as it was then quaintly called, had been handled by unadmitted clerks and was still a minority taste to be regarded with suspicion. Mann now gave it a new impulse and showed his new partners that it was not in any way *déclassé*, but on the contrary very worthwhile and its cases must be handled by a partner. And he gave the practice an international dimension.

After the merger Mann did not have to work alone. He could conduct his cases by supervising and directing small teams.   Although he was thus relieved of much of the drudgery of litigation, his colleagues were not reduced to mere foot soldiers. Those who were fortunate enough to work with him were inspired by his style of leadership and learned much that could have come from no one else.

At a time when the tide in the City firms was setting strongly towards specialisation, he swam against it. His own view was that the narrower the field of vision, the poorer the lawyer. There was hardly a subject on which he could not offer an informed and perceptive opinion. He thought everybody's door should be kept open, as his was, and that there should be a free exchange of news. He felt that if partners worked alone behind closed doors and did not discuss day-to-day problems with others, they courted danger. In the heat and pressure of a case, mistakes were liable to be made, and an outside view would ensure that the bounds of propriety were always observed. Much of his own time in the office was spent in talking to others about their cases, and giving his always trenchant, often idiosyncratic, view.

One partner who was accustomed to discuss everything with him told him one day about a current case. The client was a retired stockbroker who was sued by his former partners on an account. The defence was that the former partners were crooks, but no particulars of the malefaction could for the time being be given. The silk who had been retained specifically at the client's request had devised an ingenious method of playing for time. It transpired that Francis Mann disapproved of the silk and thought he had a reputation for unscrupulousness. (They too were divided, like the rest of humanity, into the very intelligent and honest, and the fools and the dishonest.) "You would go to this man? Why?" Mann demanded. His partner said in his own defence that he thought the choice of counsel lay with the client. There was a short pause. "Well ... you should not have such clients."

His own cases were widely spread. He conducted cases in many different jurisdictions. The *Hochschild* litigation exemplified it. This was a bitter family feud in which his client was the victim of intrigues carried on by his stepmother and associates of his elderly sick father. The war was opened up on several fronts with proceedings in Liechtenstein, the Bahamas, New York, France and London. Mann failed in his endeavours in Liechtenstein, attributable in part, he thought, to the fact that the court was made up of Swiss and Austrian judges sitting with a Liechtenstein school teacher and a farmer. But he anticipated the father's death and reckoned that the conspirators would all be staying in Paris for the funeral. In a scene which might have come out of an Ealing Studios film, he got the French proceedings on foot by having all of them served with a writ while they were breakfasting together under the chandeliers of the Hotel Meurice before attending the funeral.

Mann regretted that, with few exceptions, he had not been able to argue his own cases. International arbitrations provided him with some opportunity to do so. But, although he had a good deal of experience of arbitration, he was not generally in its favour as a method of resolving disputes. Nor was he among those who virtually made a profession of it. He thought it was usually quicker and cheaper to go to court. And his comment was that the notion that arbitration was better was "to a large extent a myth nurtured by interested persons", meaning by that, those who sponsored and promoted the idea and organised the ceaseless round of conferences on the subject.

The notorious *Barcelona Traction* case[75] was his best known opportunity to act as advocate. The case had the unusual distinction of becoming the subject of a long two-part article in the *New Yorker*.[76] Belgium had started proceedings against Spain in the International Court of Justice in The Hague. Professor Henri Rolin (in Mann's opinion, a man who enjoyed the respect of friend and enemy alike) was in charge of the Belgian case. Rolin knew the lectures that Mann had given at The Hague Academy on the doctrine of jurisdiction in international law in 1964, and invited him to join the Belgian team and to argue part of Belgium's case.

Barcelona Traction was a Canadian company with no assets or business in Spain. It operated through subsidiaries, some of which were Canadian registered companies and some Spanish. As a whole, the group was an important supplier of electricity in Spain. The group came to be controlled by Belgian interests. In 1948, associates of Juan March, Franco's financier, whose devious career is well described in the first part of the *New Yorker* article, somehow succeeded in obtaining a court order for the bankruptcy of Barcelona Traction in the small Spanish town of Reus. The next day the trustee in bankruptcy, another associate of March, took control of the whole of the group's Spanish business. In short

[75] ICJ Reports 1970, page 3.
[76] John Brooks: *Annals of Finance.* May 21 and 28, 1979.

order, the Canadian company was left an empty shell without assets or business and powerless to control its own destiny. No notice of the bankruptcy was ever given to the company. During the years that followed attempts without number were made to challenge the bankruptcy. All were unsuccessful. It was piracy by Spain against which there seemed to be no remedy. So in 1958 Belgium took the case to the International Court on behalf of the Belgian shareholders in the company. Spain asserted that the Court had no jurisdiction and that Belgium had no standing to represent a Canadian company. The Spanish Ambassador in Paris approached the Belgians and suggested meetings with March with a view to settling the dispute. The proceedings, however, would have to be discontinued first. In view of assurances given by the Ambassador, this was agreed. It was a trap. At the meeting with March it was clear that he had no intention of settling. So fresh proceedings were started. Spain raised the same objections, with the additional argument that the withdrawal of the first proceedings constituted withdrawal of the claim. In 1964 the Court rejected this last point and decided that it had jurisdiction to hear the case. Then, after some four years of work in The Hague, the Court shocked the Belgian team by deciding that Belgium had no standing.

The Court's reasoning was this. If they were proved, the wrongs were done to Barcelona Traction, a Canadian company. The Belgian nationals were its shareholders. They were separate and distinct from the company, which itself could not claim the protection of Belgium in the International Court of Justice. Mann was incensed. It was, he felt, the depths of legalism in an international dispute to pay no heed to the merits of the case. "Legal conceptualism prevailed over realism", he wrote – and shielded an act of brigandage. But he was able to have a final say. After the case, Professor Herbert Briggs, one of the members of the Spanish team, wrote an article in the American Journal of International Law analysing the decision.[77] Mann felt that he was entitled to reply and did so.[78]

In spite of his early reluctance to become a solicitor, he never looked back at that and he devoted himself to the interests of his firm until his death in 1991. In his memorial address, David Higginson, one of his closest friends in the firm, succinctly expressed the true feelings of his partners. Everything, he said, that Mann had brought to the firm was good. "Francis was a wonderful man. He filled us with wonder at what he was and what he did."

If there was one quality about him that his friends in professional life will not forget, it is that he brought excitement to the law. Lord Wilberforce thought that he somehow metamorphosed cases so that they became compelling. "So inevitably his cases were interesting", he said. "He arranged them so that they should be. And of course he almost always won, for he had devised the rule and preordained the solution. That is why working for him, or with him, was so inspiring – why he was such a joy to know."

---

[77] *65 American Journal of International Law* (1971) 327.

[78] Ibid. 67 (1973) 259; *Further Studies in International Law*, page 217.

IX

Francis Mann

Francis Mann's first and last feeling about Britain was
gratitude. The country had provided a temperate refuge
when madness raged in his own land. Owing this debt
to Britain he became a patriot. He felt that he belonged
here and was loyal and proud of being an Englishman.
The centre of his life had become firmly fixed and he
had no intention of going anywhere else. "I am British,"
he wrote, "and I owe my life and all I have become to
Britain." Any other allegiance was out of the question.
"I certainly do not wish to have any nationality other
than British, however expensive it may be." And when
a professorial colleague in Bonn asked him whether he
might take up German nationality again, he did not reply
but just looked at the questioner in a way which he had
when someone had asked something very stupid.

The second life in England supplanted the first. It
was not so much that his German childhood and youth
disappeared behind his new identity, but that he put it
into a watertight compartment in his mind. In England
he never talked about it or the circumstances that had
brought it to an end. He never read about the Holocaust.
But he went willingly to Berlin after the war and searched
for traces of the life that had been. It is impossible to say
what he really felt about the lost years, but it is certain that
they were replaced by a new loyalty and a new affection.
Lord Hoffmann, who knew him and went to concerts

with him only in his last four or five years, thought that he had become thoroughly English – with a German accent. He had severed his connection with Germany, or rather Germany had severed it and he had accepted it. When he went back to teach it was as a visiting professor from abroad. And in his admiration for the common law system he had the zeal of the convert, constantly warning about the malign influence of the continent. And not only in the legal sphere.

Although he was a man of wide European culture, he was a consistent opponent of closer European union. He distrusted a common European currency precisely because it would inevitably lead to a European state. He was profoundly sceptical that the original purpose of the founders of the European movement could be realised. Why should a political union prevent another war on the continent? Like his political heroine, Margaret Thatcher, he did not think that bringing Germany into a European union with its neighbours would achieve a permanent peace on the continent. On the contrary, Germany's economic dynamism would make it the dominant force in the European Community and a destabilising influence. Mann admired Mrs Thatcher for saying so with clarity, and not, as Sir Percy Cradock, her foreign policy adviser, said of other Western leaders, sharing her concerns but composing their features and saying very different things in public.[79] Mann remained almost fatalistically suspicious of German ambitions throughout his life.

Mann's reasons for going back to Germany to teach were explained by the former Dean of the Law Faculty at the University of Bonn, Professor H H Jakobs, when he paid his *in memoriam* tribute:

[79] Documents on British Policy Overseas, Series III, Volume VII, Preface, pages xv, xxxiii.

Not in order to belong to Germany, and not in order to be an English *and* a German lawyer and thereby one of us, did he make the effort to lecture in Bonn and to share his thoughts with people in Germany. It seems to me now that he wanted to demonstrate to us how poor that materially wealthy country Germany really is, and how much this country lost after 1933 which it never gained back after 1945, so that the world does not respect her but fears her and has good reason for doing so.

Mann succeeded triumphantly in this vocation. He lectured all over Germany until in 1960 he was appointed Honorary Professor at Bonn where each summer he gave a course of lectures. He wrote frequently in the German legal periodicals and once in a while in the newspapers. *The Legal Aspect of Money* was published in a German translation. The German Federal Republic recognised his achievements open-handedly. In 1977 the President conferred the Grand Cross of the Order of Merit on him and a *Festschrift* was published in his honour. The University of Kiel granted him an honorary doctorate and at Bonn a great celebration was organised to mark the fiftieth anniversary of his Berlin doctorate.

But perhaps his greatest satisfaction, the piquancy of which is easy to appreciate, came from his being asked by the Federal Republic to act as its advocate in an arcane case arising out of the "Young Loan". This was the agreement made in 1930 between Germany and the Allies to rationalise the German external debt, reduced to a chaotic state by the burden of reparations imposed by the Treaty of Versailles. The creditor powers were unable to agree with the Federal Republic whether the upward revaluations of the Deutsche Mark in 1961 and 1969 should result in a re-calculation of the external debt, so the issue had to go to arbitration. Mann's argument that no re-calculation should be made succeeded by a narrow majority.[80]

But for all his success in Germany, he doubted whether he had after all been able to exert a real influence. Had he done anything to help recreate a new impression of the Jew on the mind of Germany, one that looked back across the abyss to the age of enlightenment he had known? A new generation of Germans had grown up. They did not know what had happened. They did not want to know. At best the appalling history of those twelve years was an abstraction, just safely beyond the range of memory. And he feared the recrudescence of the German will to mastery. Not in his time or even his grandchildren's, but some time. It was, he thought, something in the dark soul of the country, and it would out. "How could this happen in the full light of day, and why was it just the German people from whom this great evil sprang?" asked the Israeli District Court in the Eichmann trial. Mann did not harbour these forebodings alone. His German colleagues in Bonn, some of them his contemporaries, shared them. And Helmut Kohl had gone to Belgium, a country loaded with historical memory, to plead for a closer European union that would bind Germany in, and prevent her from giving rein to those tendencies that her neighbours had reason to dread. Mann's feelings for the country of his birth were bound to be equivocal. The pain of loss had gone deep. He seemed to lock it away separately where it could not spread to his English identity. Perhaps it made him more pessimistic than he need have been.

Loyal though they were to the country of their adoption, Francis and Lore Mann never lost the feeling of being

---

[80] 59 Int.LR (1980) 494; *The Legal Aspect of Money* (5th edition) page 62.

immigrants. In the early days when their friends were few, Lore was once asked, whom did she know? Only the Forsytes, she said. They could not lose their accent. It was a burden and one of the reasons why Francis did not go to the Bar. Lore also did not like to stand up and speak in the County and Magistrates' courts in her poor persons' legal practice. They decided that they would not settle in the north-west corridor of London, the traditional home of the Jewish middle class. Their early homes were there, in St. John's Wood and nearby, but when the time came to buy a house, they chose Addison Avenue in Holland Park. They chose not to live where there was a high proportion of Jews. That was not the way their own assimilated families had lived in Germany, and not the way they brought up their own children. The children grew up in every respect as English children. The two girls went to St. Paul's and then Cambridge. David went to Stowe and Oxford. Both Francis and Lore Mann refused to compromise about education, despite Lore's egalitarian views. It would have been unthinkable for them to conceal their Jewishness – on the contrary they were proud of it – but they disliked ostentatious parade, and they were not at ease with the pious traditions of Judaism. Because they did not go to the synagogue or keep the festivals, they had no natural community. The only known occasion when Mann went to a synagogue was on the day the war in Europe ended. He was elated and felt a need to give thanks in the sanctuary. The Rabbi greeted him warmly and invited him to read a Hebrew prayer to the congregation. He fled in terror.

The treatment Mann received at the hands of the academic establishment in England only served to confirm his feeling of being an outsider. In 1945 Arthur Goodhart, the anglophile American jurist, Master of University

College, Oxford and a long-time supporter, offered him a Fellowship at the College. But he could not possibly support his family on the stipend. Then in 1949 an incident occurred which left a permanent mark of resentment. He applied for the chair of International Law at London University. His sponsors were illustrious: Dr Geoffrey Cheshire, Sir Hersch Lauterpacht and Sir Valentine Holmes. There was a short list of three. The appointing committee included Lord McNair and Sir David Hughes Parry. No appointment was made. The chair remained unfilled for another ten years. No one on the short list was appointed and no explanation given for the extraordinary way of going on. Mann heard later, perhaps a rumour, that it might be unwise to appoint a foreigner ... therefore it was better to make no appointment at all. The story is credible but unproven. Mann had a thin skin, his disappointment was acute, and it rankled.

His strong patriotism for Britain did not mean that he was uncritical. The weakness of the intelligentsia, the men of the left and many others of liberal tendency, and their unwillingness to face unpleasant facts, had endangered Britain during the thirties. It caused Mann grief and anger. In 1980, with the affair of Anthony Blunt, it surfaced again. In November 1979 Mrs Thatcher made a statement in the House of Commons about Blunt, who then held an appointment in the Royal Household as Surveyor of the Queen's Pictures.[81] He had, said the Prime Minister, been recruited by the USSR as a spy while he was an undergraduate at Cambridge before the war. In 1940 he had joined the British security service and had remained in post there until 1945. During that time he had regularly passed information to Russian

[81] 974 Hansard (5th Series) col. 402 (21 November 1979).

intelligence.   After 1945 he had resumed his career as
an art historian.   He had made a full confession and
been offered immunity from prosecution.   He was later
stripped of his knighthood.

Blunt was a Fellow of the British Academy, as was Mann.
In July 1980, the Annual General Meeting of the Academy
had to consider a recommendation from its Council that
Blunt be expelled on the ground of his treachery.   An
alternative motion proposed that the Academy "deplore"
Blunt's activities but take no further action.   After some
debate the meeting accepted by 120 votes to 42 a third
motion simply "to proceed to the next business."   Mann
was not able to be present at the meeting, but he made
it clear that if Blunt had not subsequently resigned – as
happened – Mann would have done so himself.   He and
others like Robert Blake, the historian, were outraged by
the behaviour of the Fellows at the meeting.   Blake's view
was that it was impossible for the Academy to ignore
political or moral behaviour, and take the view that the
only ground for expelling a Fellow was a purely academic
offence like plagiarism.   He added that he thought that
many academics had leftward leanings and a sneaking
sympathy with those who had helped the USSR.   "Pink
liberal jellies" was his name for them.   A J P Taylor, the
historian, was among those who thought that selling
secrets to the Russians was not a good reason for expelling
Blunt from a purely academic institution.   Mann's son-in-
law, Professor Charles Thomas, who later became a Fellow
himself, encapsulated the view that Blunt ought to have
been expelled, by commenting that it seemed that "Blunt's
contributions to Caravaggio, etc., greatly outweighed a
little spare-time treason."[82]   *The Times*, whose editorial

---

[82] Private communications from Lord Blake and Professor Charles
Thomas.

policy was perennially suspect on this issue, declared in its leader on 22 August 1980 that "Mr Taylor was right to point to the dangers of allowing any consideration other than academic distinction to influence the selection of Fellows." Mann wrote a letter of protest to *The Times* but the editor declined to publish it.

There the matter might have rested, had not there been further debate in the columns of *Encounter*. For reasons which are obscure, Sir Kenneth Dover, the President of the Academy,[83] wrote a long and jesuitical explanation (much of it guesswork) in the November 1980 issue of the conduct of Fellows at the Annual General Meeting, He neither condemned nor excused the decision to do nothing about Blunt. He could see the arguments on both sides and was quite ready to advocate either. A J P Taylor followed in the June 1981 issue. He thought it odd that Sir Kenneth appeared to have no view. For his part, he considered it a matter of high principle and if Blunt had been expelled, he would have resigned himself. He thought that Blunt had been forced into resigning as a result of a witch-hunt, and as a consequence he, Taylor, then resigned. The debate having been resumed, Mann felt entitled to publish his own deeply held views (*Encounter*, September 1981). His letter deserves to be given in full:

> Mr A J P Taylor and Sir Kenneth Dover disclaim any intention to revive the Blunt affair. But having done so, they must put up with a reply by a Fellow of the British Academy who unfortunately was unable to attend last year's Annual General Meeting and who ever since has considered the Academy's failure to expel Blunt as one of the most discreditable incidents of recent academic history in Britain.

---

[83] Unfortunately, Sir Kenneth Dover embargoed the Blunt file in the Academy's records during his own lifetime.

First, as to the law. According to Rule 11 of the Bye-laws the AGM "may remove the name of any person from the list of Fellows on the ground that he or she is not a fit and proper person to be a Fellow." The words are not subject to any qualification. They cannot be understood as limiting the power of removal to grounds appertaining to scholarship, as Rule 27 relating to elections seems, but cannot intend, to do; for it is impossible to believe that it is open to the Council to nominate for election a person who has been convicted of or has confessed to a serious crime, let alone one of the most serious crimes of all, viz. treason. But even if Rule 27, by its reference to Article 6 of the Charter, should contemplate exclusively academic achievements, the absence of any such reference in Rule 11 underlines the generality of the power of removal.

However this may be, it is distressing to learn from Mr Taylor's letter that in voting against the expulsion of Blunt he believed he was acting as one of "the defenders of intellectual liberty." This involves a confusion of frightening dimensions. Is it suggested that intellectual liberty implies the right to commit treason or that treason is the justifiable product of intellectual liberty? Can it seriously be thought that a spy and traitor necessarily acts in defence of intellectual liberty? Have we so completely forgotten the meaning of language as to be unable to distinguish between crime and motive (though we know nothing whatever about the true character of Blunt's motives)? Can it reasonably be believed that if Blunt's misdeeds had been known in 1955 he would have been elected or anybody would have ventured to propose him?

One of the most painful aspects of the Blunt affair (which, if he had not resigned, would have compelled me to leave so mealy-mouthed a body as the British Academy in 1980) is the lack of moral fibre which the vote at the AGM disclosed. Can we no longer recognise and condemn a crime, when it is admitted and plain to see? Must I, or a foreign Corresponding Fellow, or one of our Honorary Fellows at the annual dinner sit next to a self-confessed criminal? Is there, for purposes of membership, any difference between a traitor, a murderer, or a thief? (There is a hint at *l'affaire Dreyfus* in Mr Taylor's letter; but Dreyfus was innocent, Blunt admitted to be guilty.)

I shall defend real "intellectual liberty" to the last, but I deny the right of anyone to call treason an act of intellectual liberty or a man "fit and proper" for membership of the British Academy merely because he is academically distinguished. This is a matter, not of party, or institutional politics, but of common sense and very elementary moral values. It is paradoxical that by his resignation a traitor enabled the Academy to maintain them.

After the relief of victory in 1945 and all the hope invested in the post-war future, Mann was forced to watch Britain's slow, irreversible decline. It was made more painful by the gratitude he felt for what the country had done for him and his family. But he was able to give it an ironic sideways look. What can I do about it? He often said. And later in life he used to add: I am an old man on the way out. Nevertheless, the steepness of the downward slope affected his political view. Always inclined to the right, the Labour government which succeeded the wartime coalition gave his natural tendency a sharp impulse. The Attlee administration, in his view, had abused the promise that had been won by victory. The effort of the war had admittedly impoverished the country's resources, but its morale and prestige in the world were high, and the opportunity for greatness in peace as in war was there for the taking. Yet all was squandered. Within thirty years Britain had become a poor and backward country, obsessed with trivia and nostalgia for the past, overtaken by its defeated enemies. And after forty years, the appetite for trivia was still increasing. "I am having what people say is a good time", he wrote in his usual pithy style to his secretary from his summer retreat in Sils Maria in the Engadine in 1986, "but looked at from here England is mad and preoccupied with pettiness."

In Mann's view, the origins of the decline were to be traced to the Labour government. It was they who had imposed currency controls to create a humiliating siege economy, and it was they who had enslaved the nation to the irresponsible power of the unions. In that first post-war administration England had made a shameful conquest of itself. No wonder that he welcomed the coming of Margaret Thatcher, who was to take on and defeat one by one all the bugbears that had dogged Britain's progress since the war. His admiration for her never dimmed, not even in the hubris of her last years. But it was an irony that he may have perceived that it was Mrs Thatcher who first lit the fuse under the restrictive practices ruling in the legal profession – the practices which were an integral part of the profession he felt so passionately should be left exactly as it was. The lament for national decline is familiar, and his own version of it was simplistic. Nonetheless it contained much that was true. The history of post-war Britain seemed incomprehensible to those, like Mann, who had seen and admired its greatness.

The English terrain in which Mann felt at home was that of the professional middle classes, the segment of society that corresponded most nearly to the society in Germany which he had been forced to relinquish. After the war their natural conservatism was tinged, as was his, with nostalgia. One of their favourite authors, as his, was Anthony Trollope, who could conjure the sweetness of the lost world. As Mann moved right, his wife moved away towards an egalitarianism and a simplicity that was also puritan and could be censorious. As his increasing affluence enabled him to indulge his (still moderate) taste for luxurious hotels and good wine, she came to think of all privilege as sordid.

In 1955 she was admitted as a solicitor and at last
began the legal career that had been denied her in 1933.
The children were of an age when she could make the
necessary time. But even when she was busiest she was
always at home for her children and her husband. He
never came home to an empty house and never cooked
for himself – although it was unlikely that he could have
boiled an egg even in dire emergency. As he happily
admitted, she did everything for him. He had only to
glance at newspapers and magazines, relying on her to
tell him about books, theatres and other news that she
thought he ought to know about or be interested in.
"This all-embracing knowledge had a serious effect on
me. I came to appreciate it to the full extent only after
her death," he wrote – for all husbands of self-sacrificing
wives.

She decided to dedicate herself to helping the poor.
She worked as an assistant solicitor for two small firms
in West London, and then in September 1966 she took
over the practice of Goodwin and Knipe at 204 Portobello
Road. That street then had none of the fashionable
tourist cachet which it now has. It was a rough area with
a population predominantly from the Caribbean. It was
here in Notting Hill that Britain had its first experience
of a multi-racial society; and here that she launched her
pioneering poor law practice. Only months later, in May
1967, her first assistant, Barbara Thomson, was in her
last term at school awaiting the results of the university
clearing system when she read an advertisement in the
New Statesman. It invited applications for an assistant
or articled clerk in the Portobello Road practice. She
applied and went for an interview. It was the first time she
had seen a really run-down area and she was shaken. But
she gritted her teeth and got the job. She took her articles

with Lore and stayed, in the later years after the birth of her children on a part-time basis, until 1982, after Lore's death. In all that time there was only one unpleasant incident. The husband of a client came into the office and started to push Barbara about. The shopkeeper from the ground floor heard the commotion, came up, and saw the man off in a good-humoured way. Barbara Thomson's successor was Sabiha Hasan, who had come to Britain from Pakistan as a child. She was qualified when she joined the practice in 1976 and, as Lore wished, took over the practice when Lore died, subsequently becoming a District Court judge.

Lore Mann was a feminist and would not have a man working in the office. Nor would she act for a man in a matrimonial case. "All men are mad" was one of her most frequent dicta. A high proportion of the cases were for battered or deserted wives and their children. West Indian fathers enforced discipline by beating. But there were no cases of child abuse. Almost all were legally aided. Lore taught by example, having her assistant in the room while the client was being interviewed and explaining exactly what was happening in her presence. Both her assistants recalled her as absolutely direct and straight. Her manner was brusque but it hid her shyness. She was kind and protective to both girls and took time to talk to them. Barbara Thomson had heard much about Lore's husband and expected something of a luxury-loving tyrant who made his wife do everything; she was surprised to find that he was utterly charming when she met him, and could well understand how he had made the work in Portobello Road possible by financing it out of his own earnings. For his part, he was astonished almost nightly by the stories his wife brought home of a world he knew nothing of and could barely imagine.

This extraordinary practice was the first of its kind, before Neighbourhood Law Centres were thought of, and she was a true professional who was superb at the work. After her death, one of the stall-holders from the street market told Barbara Thomson that "she had the respect of the market."

Lore did not share her husband's interest in post-war Germany or his desire to help. He thought that there was nothing more the Germans could have done to atone, and he admired much of what they had done, particularly the work of the courts in striking down Nazi laws. The post-war courts in Germany were particularly tender to Jewish litigants who, said one of his friends, were protected like ancient monuments. Her attitude was more typical of the Jewish refugees than his. For her, nothing could atone. She had always been the more uncompromising.

But when it came to integrity, there was nothing to choose between them. Both were unflinching. His views about law and lawlessness never yielded to circumstance, however hard the case. This led him into some extreme positions. He condemned the Allies' taking of German-owned property in Switzerland in 1946 for the purpose of helping to repair the ravages of Nazism, when the commonly held view was that the confiscation was richly justified. And he considered that the forcible abduction of Eichmann from Argentina had vitiated his subsequent trial in Jerusalem. "However revolting and unique Eichmann's crimes were and however desirable it was to bring him to justice," he wrote, "a deliberate breach of international law remains unpardonable."[84] In a review of a book on the trial, he was more explicit. "Was not one

---

[84] *The Doctrine of Jurisdiction in International Law.* In *Studies in International Law*, page 113, footnote 6.

of the most effective arguments against execution to be derived from the breach of international law which Israel herself had committed and without which she could not have asserted the supremacy of the law?"[85]

His views on Israel were unusual ones for a Jew to hold. Some thought them exaggerated or even perverse. But they were part of a coherent view that lawlessness is always the same, no matter by whose hand violence is done: it is never to be condoned or explained away. In the summer of 1946, in the last tragic phase of the British mandate in Palestine and while he was working in Berlin with the Allied Control Council, Jewish terrorists declared open war on the British. In July the King David Hotel in Jerusalem was blown up and 90 people were killed. He wrote home about it. He was sure that the Jewish Agency had instigated, supported and shielded the terrorists. He condemned it, he told Lore, as severely as he condemned the Nazis. "So long as this continues, the Jewish Agency, representing Zionism, must share the blame. It is essential to stick to moral values, and if one fails, as the Jewish Agency has done, one forfeits the right to complain."

These events seem to have inclined Mann's heart permanently. As the sequence of events led on to the British withdrawal and the bloody birth of Israel he could never forget that the founders of the state were implicated in criminal violence: men whom he thought of as having failed to seize a historic opportunity to make a shared land and a wider union of Arab and Jew. Some of his closest friends who had sought refuge in Palestine in the thirties returned hurriedly to Germany in 1948. He

---

[85] 28 *Modern Law Review* (1965) 379. Review of *The Eichmann Trial:* Papadatos: Stevens 1964.

agreed with their reasons. The invasion of Lebanon in 1982 outraged him more than any other event in Israel's history. After the massacres in the Palestinian refugee camps at Chatila and Sabra, in which accusations were made, but never substantiated, of Israeli complicity, he wrote to The Times to comment on the reported request by Israel to the United States for a record amount of aid. "If the U S should be prepared to give any aid to Israel, should not payment be made to Lebanon in part settlement of Israel's liability for reparations?"[86]   He was never a true sympathiser with Israel or, after the Jewish State had been established, a friend to the Zionist organisations.

In the autumn of 1980 it became clear that Lore's health was failing. She refused to see a doctor: apart from attendance by gynaecologists during her pregnancies she had not consulted a doctor since 1934. She thought of medical attention as an indignity. Finally, in November she agreed to see the family doctor who was also one of their closest friends. She had lost most of her blood. She had transfusions and further tests were carried out. Cancer of the colon was diagnosed and an operation would be necessary. She tidied up her affairs and went to a hotel where she took an overdose and fell asleep reading.

She had often spoken approvingly of euthanasia and made it transparently clear that she could not face being a burden to anyone or living the life of an invalid without control over her own life. Her husband had never quite accepted the literalness of that, and he recalled the "almost whimsical" expression in her face when she was being urged to see a doctor. But when it had

---

[86] *The Times* 18 October 1982.

happened and the first devastation of shock had passed, he recognised that she had lived and died according to her own unbending principles. There was, he afterwards wrote, a classical stoicism about her. He asked himself whether there was not an element of selfishness. But, he acknowledged, in truth she was the most unselfish of persons, concerning herself constantly with the welfare of her children and with the plight of the poor. In the end she was the professional woman that in her heart she had wanted to be since her time in Berlin. She too had led a double life, in her home and in her work. Her husband knew the debt he owed her. It was she who had made possible what he called his own double life – of practice and writing. She had relieved him of all work in the house and had made no demands on his time. He summed it up: "She respected, promoted and supported the curious life I had to lead to give it the quality it had."

After his wife died, Francis Mann moved to a pleasant flat in Manchester Street, just behind Oxford Street, and lived there for the remaining eleven years of his life. He continued to go to the office every day just as if he were a partner, although he had become a consultant. It suited him that way. He was bored by administration. He continued to write frequently for the legal periodicals and he prepared the 5th edition of *The Legal Aspect of Money* up to the point of proof reading for publication. Although he was lonely, like many widows and widowers he found the freedom to do what he liked when he liked not unwelcome. He went to concerts with friends and took an annual summer holiday in the Engadine. Here, among the woods and mountains for which he cherished a long-time affection, he stayed in a gloomy hotel with a group of friends some of whom went back to his Berlin days. The last links with the old Europe. They took gentle walks in the woods, drank some wine and talked sometimes of the old days. One walk which was perfectly level was known among them as the *Boulevard des Invalides.*

He visited Hong Kong which he thought "probably the most fabulous place I have ever seen" and told his secretary in a post card that she would adore it. He hoped she was having a good time "while I am not bothering you". He went to Hawaii but, as could have been predicted, it was "not for me". "Looked at from here", he said, as he always did when he was away from home, "the English seem to be mad, madder than ever".

He continued to take his regular Sunday morning walks in the Park with Michael Kerr and Mark Littman, and then repaired to the Littmans for lunch. Marguerite Littman looked forward to his visits. He liked to be teased and he never failed to notice and compliment her on what she was wearing. He brought oxygen into the room, she said. Estelle Spottiswoode had known and admired the Manns since her husband, Derek, equally an admirer, joined Hardman, Phillips and Mann in 1951. Her abiding memory of Francis was of a man of energy, warmth and simplicity: he went to the heart of the matter. On his side, Mann greatly enjoyed the company of women and visibly appreciated good looks until the day of his death. He admired too their practical good sense and their directness. In the ruins of Berlin in 1946 he had found that it was the women who had the greater strength and who had better preserved their dignity through the unspeakable experiences they had suffered. He was not surprised that it was a woman who had supplied the leadership which had been missing in Britain since Churchill's day.

Francis Mann loved his children and his grandchildren

– although he did not at all love the noise and chaos that is inseparable from very small children. Always a generous man, he showed it particularly towards his grandchildren, helping with their school fees and in many other ways. He enjoyed conversation with children when they were of an age to sustain a discussion, and never talked down to them: what they said mattered. He enjoyed too his patriarchal role among his many offspring and took great pride in their achievements. For their part his worldly wisdom, warmth and inimitable humour delighted them.

He did not undervalue his own work, and he was not entirely without the vanity which can sometimes walk with achievement. He possessed too the "academic pride" to which he had confessed to his wife in a letter from Berlin in 1946. When it came to intellectual intercourse he chose his friends carefully, and did not suffer fools gladly – or at all. The world was divided into the intelligent and "complete fools", as he often described those unfortunates. He was a good hater. There was quite a long list of academics who had earned his contempt or animosity. One of these appeared once in a Swiss resort where Mann was staying. He as quickly disappeared. "Am I wrong?" Mann demanded of a friend who was also there and who had questioned his behaviour. "Then why should I not say it?" But although it might seem so, the certainty with which he held a legal opinion and the impatience he had with other views or, even more, with blurry qualifications, was not arrogance. It was simply that he saw it with absolute clarity. His intellect had the quality of decision.

The English academic establishment eventually recognised Francis Mann's distinction. He was elected a Fellow of the British Academy in 1974, and then in 1980 he was awarded the CBE for services to international law and was gratified by the thought that the honour meant more for an immigrant. In 1989 he received an Honorary Doctorate from Oxford. In the last year of his life he became the first practising solicitor to be made an honorary Queen's Counsel, and in the same year he became an honorary Bencher of Gray's Inn. His friends in Bonn were understandably baffled by some of the titles their friend was collecting in England, particularly that of "honorary Bencher". As they were sitting together one summer evening on a terrace overlooking the Rhine, they asked him what it meant, and whether there were any special rights attached to the honour. "Certainly: it means you sit on the Bench." That did not seem to carry the matter further so they pressed him: "Sit on the Bench?" They were made to feel that it was a stupid question and one which he had already answered. "What should it mean? You sit on the Bench!" But after a moment he relented. "Well, my friends, you have to remember: not bad for a bloody foreigner."

In 1980 Lord Denning paid him a famous compliment. "Of all my learned friends, Francis Mann is the most learned of all", he wrote in the introduction to his book, *The Due Process of Law*. Then two years later, in writing to the senior partner of Herbert Smith on the occasion of the firm's centenary celebrations, he paid Mann a further compliment that was perhaps more perceptive, and was certainly overwhelming. "Thank you exceedingly for the splendid occasion", Denning wrote. "It must be recorded in your annals. And how fortunate I was to be seated next to your good Francis Mann who has contributed more than anyone to the development of the science of law in our time." Mann's long affair with the English legal system never cooled. What Denning admired was his unique contribution. For he brought to it not only the enthusiasm of the outsider who had come in, but also the learning and order which he had carried with him from Germany. For Mann, Denning was his greatest encourager and his friendship with the great judge meant more to him than formal honours.

Francis Mann considered that the modest lesson life had taught him is that there is time for everything. He confessed that much that the Englishman might want to do did not interest him. No one should be surprised to learn that ball games and gardening (which in a characteristic aside he remarked could better be done by a gardener) were among them. But, he wrote, "if you organise your life intelligently there is nothing you cannot achieve – lack of time usually is an excuse rather than a reality." Those who remember the energy he possessed until his dying day can only humbly agree.